EADWELL'S

LEAR
IN A MONTH

Easy Method of Learning Nepali
Through English Without a Teacher

By :

N.K. Guha

Readwell Publications
NEW DELHI-110008

Published by :
READWELL PUBLICATIONS
B-8, Rattan Jyoti, 18, Rajendra Place
New Delhi-110 008 (INDIA)
Phone : 5737448, 5712649, 5721761
Fax : 91-11-5812385
E-mail : readwell@sify.com
newlight@vsnl.net

ISBN 81-87782-12-9

Printed at : Arya Offset Press, New Delhi.

CONTENTS

Preface

The Nepali language is very dear to our people and there are good reasons for it. First, the alphabet of Nepali is the same as that of Hindi. The grammar of both is similar and the syntax shows no historical variance. Besides, the cultural and historical affinities between the two countries have drawn the people to this language and this is the foremost reason why the Nepali language is treated here as one of its own langauges. The open border between the two countries lends still greater urgency to the desire for learning this language.

Large numbers of people visit Nepal for business, sight-seeing or any other reason and they feel handicapped by lack of knowledge of Nepali. It is in view of this need that we have brought forth this small work. The scheme of this book is very clear and it has been made a narrative type. The lessons on grammar and syntax have been made very easy and nothing has been left unexplained.

We will consider ourselves rewarded if the people accept it and derive full benefit from it. We will be open to constructive criticism or suggestions for improving upon this humble work and shall gladly accept them.

AUTHOR

Publisher's Note

We present this book—"Learn Nepali in a month through English"—for the convenience of businessmen, educationists, students and foreigners.

Every effort has been made to make it a simple reading and interesting book for easy grasp of the language.

As it is very akin to the Hindi language, the Nepali and Hindi speaking students can easily make a breakthrough and pick up the flowers in the garden of Nepali language with the minimum effort and within the shortest possible time.

Nepal abounds in natural beauties all around—hills and dale—rivers and mountains—forests and plain. These have equally enriched her language in tune with its culture and music—region and customs and the readers will enjoy the Nepali language a great deal.

LESSON—I
How to write & pronounce Alphabets
VOWELS & CONSONANTS

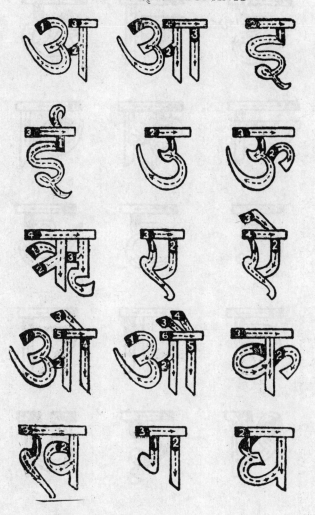

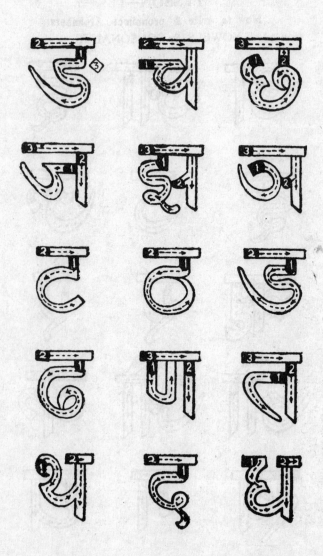

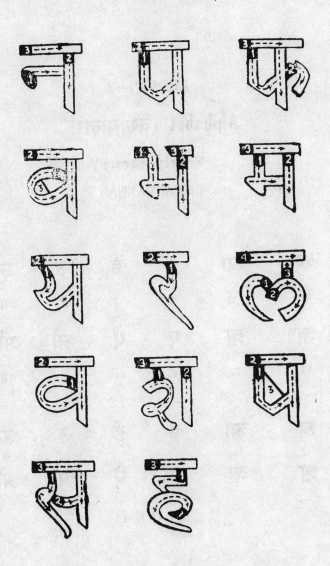

LESSON—2

Alphabet (वर्णमाला)

Vowels (स्वरवर्ण)

[SWARVARNA]

अ	आ	इ	ई	उ	ऊ
a	a	i	i	u	u

ऋ	ॠ	ए	ऐ	ओ	औ
ri	ri	e	ai	o	au

अ	आ	इ	ई	उ	ऊ
ऋ	ॠ	ए	ऐ	ओ	औ

Read :—

इ ए ऋ ओ ऊ ऋ

ॠ ई ऐ उ ओ आ

The letters अ आ ओ औ are also written as
अ आ ओ औ respectively; so both the forms
should be known.

Vowels are of two kinds :—

      (i)   short (ह्रस्व—hraswa) ; and
      (ii) long (दीर्घ—dirgha).

(i) short vowels (hraswa-swar) are :—

अ   इ   उ   ऋ
a   i   u   ri

(ii) long vowels (dirgha-swar) are :—

आ ई ऊ ॠ ए ऐ ओ औ
a i u ri e ai o au

Short vowels are to be pronounced short
and long vowels long.

The forms of the vowels just given are mostly
used at the beginning of a word. They have

short forms also, as given below. The shorter form of a vowel may be called the consonantal form. The general name matra (मात्रा) is given to the short form.

अ (a) has no short form; the letter is omitted when used with a consonant.

आ	becomes	ा	and is called			akar.
इ	,,	ि	,,	,,		ikar
ई	,,	ी	,,	,,		ikar
	,,	ु	,,	,,		ukar
ऊ	,,	ू	,,	,,		ukar
ऋ	,,	ृ	,,	,,		rikar
ॠ	,,	ॄ	,,	,,		rikar
ए	,,	े	,,	,,		ekar
ऐ	,,	ै	,,	,,		ekar
ओ	,,	ो	,,	,,		okar
औ	,,	ौ	,,	,,		aukar

———

CONSONANTS (व्यंजनवर्ण)
(*Vyanjan-varna*)

अ (a) is inherent in every consonant sound but while pronouncing words this Final Vowel sound is often dropped.

क्	ख्	ग्	घ्	ङ्
k	kh	g	gh	n

क	ख	ग	घ	ङ		च	छ	ज	झ	ञ
ka	kha	ga	gha	na		cha	chha	ja	jha	na

ट	ठ	ड	ढ	ण		त	थ	द	ध	न
ta	tha	da	dha	na		ta	tha	da	dha	na

प	फ	ब	भ	म		य	र	ल	व	श
pa	pha	ba	bha	ma		ya	ra	la	va	sa

ष	स	ह		ः
sa	sa	ha	m	h	-

If a consonant has to be written where the vowel अ is not blended with it, a sign (्) called *hal* (हल्) is used ; as—क्+अ=क, ख्+अ=ख ; etc.

क ख ग घ ङ   च छ ज झ ञ

ट ठ ड ढ ण   त थ द ध न

प फ ब भ म   य र ल व श

ष स ह ः

Read :—

ग ल ब क ध   झ च ख ङ ज

त छ ट ज ः   व घ श भ ,

न थ ण ठ य फ र ष ह ढ

व स म   ड प

The letters झ, ग, ल, are also written as झ ग, ल, respectively; so both the forms should be known.

Read :—

ग्रब (ab)—now   तब (tab) - then

जब (jab)—when   घर (ghar)—house

सब (sab)—all   फल (phal)—fruit

एक (ek)—one   तर (tar) – but

Now comes the writing process of the letters. All the letters should be written from left to right. The starting points are marked with serial numbers. The learners should follow the directions given in the following pages for easy and correct writing.

LESSON—3

VOWEL-SIGNS (स्वर-चिह्नहरू)

(Swar-Chinhaharu)

The use of Vowel-signs with consonants :—

क् + आ (ा) = का (ka)

क् + इ (ि) = कि (ki)

क् + ई (ी) = की (ki)

क् + उ (ु) = कु (ku)

क् + ऊ (ू) = कू (ku)

क् + ऋ (ृ) = कृ (kri)

क् + ॠ (ॄ) = कृ (kri)

क् + ए (े) = के (ke)

क् + ऐ (ै) = कै (kai)

क् + ओ (ो) = को (ko)

क् + औ (ौ) = कौ (kau)

क् + अं (ं) = कं (kam)

क् + अः (:) = कः (kah)

क् + अँ (ँ) = कँ (kan)

Note :—The sings of श्रा, ई, श्रो, श्रो (ा, ी, ा, are placed after the consonants; the sign of इ (before the consonants ; उ, ऊ ऋ, ॠ (ुूृ immediately under the consonants and ए, ऐ (ॆ above the consonants.

Read :—

यता जाऊ (eta au)—Come here.

उता जाऊ (uta jau)— Go there.

श्रालु खाऊ (alu khau)—Eat the potato.

कमीज ल्याऊ (kamij lyau)—Bring shirt.

धागो कात (dhago kata) —Spin yarn.

कपड़ा बुन (kapada buna)—Weave cloth.

किताब पढ़(kitab padha)—Read the book.

There are twelve different forms of writing a consonant according to the vowel-sign it is joined with. The following are the twelve different forms and they are called barha khari (बा-ह्र खरी) in Nepali

VOWEL-SIGNS (स्वर–चिह्नहरू)

क––का	कि	का	कु	कू	कृ
ka ka	ki	ki	ku	ku	kri
के	कै	को	कौ	कं	कः
ke	kai	ko	kau	kam	kah

ख––खा	खि	खो	खु	खू	खृ
kha kha	khi	khi	khu	khu	khri
खे	खै	खों	खौ	खं	खः
khe	khai	kho	khau	kham	khah

ग–– गा	गि	गो	गु	गू	गृ
ga ga	gi	gi	gu	gu	gri
गे	गै	गो	गौ	गं	गः
ge	gai	go	gau	gam	gah

घ–– घा	घि	घो	घु	घू	घृ
gha gha	ghi	ghi	ghu	ghu	ghri
घे	घै	घों	घौं	घं	घः
ghe	ghai	gho	ghau	gham	ghah

न––चा	चि	चो	चु	चू	चृ
hac cha	chi	chi	chu	chu	chri

चे	चै	चों	चौ	चं	चः
che	chai	cho	chau	cham	chan

छ——छा	छि	छी	छु	छू	छृ
chha-chha	chhi	chhi	chhu	chhu	chhri

छे	छै	छो	छौ	छं	छः
chhe	chhai	chho	chhau	chham	chhah

ज——जा	जि	जी	जु	जू	जृ
ja—	ja	ji	ji	ju	ju	jri

जे	जै	जो	जौ	जं	जः
je	jai	jo	jau	jam	jah

झ——झा	झि	झी	झु	झू	झः
jha—jha	jhi	jhi	jhu	jhu	jhri

झे	झै	झो	झौ	झं	झः
jhe	jhai	jho	jhau	jham	jhah

ट——टा	टि	टी	टु	टू	टृ
ta—	ta	ti	ti	tu	tu	tri

टे	टै	टो	टौ	टं	टः
te	tai	to	tau	tam	tah

Vowel signs are used in the same way with
all the consonants excepting उ and ऊ with र ; as —

र + उ = रु ; र + ऊ = रू ।

VOWEL-SIGNS (स्वर.चिह्नहरू)

Read :—

आ (ा)	बाबू (babu) father	काका (kaka) uncle
इ (ि)	दिन (din) day	किताब (kitab) book
ई (ी)	घडी (ghadi) clock	पानी (pani) water
उ (ु)	पुरानो (purano) old	गुरू (guru) preceptor
ऊ (ू)	पूजा (puja) worship	रूप (rupa) form
ऋ (ृ)	कृपा (kripa) kindness	ऋण (rina) debt
ए (े)	सेवा (seva) service	तेल (tel) oil
ऐ (ै)	पैसा (paisa) pice	मैला (maila) garbage
ओ (ो)	रोटी (roti) bread	मोटा (mota) fat
औ (ौ)	कौ (kau) blacksmith	नौनी (nauni) butter

अं (ं)	अंश (amsa) part	सिंह (simha) lion
अः (ः)	दुःख (duhkha) sorrow	पुन : (punah) again
अँ (ँ)	कहाँ (kahan) where	दांत (dant) tooth

Note:— The half nasal sound ँ (chandravindu) is used only when there is no vowel sign on the top of the letter; as :— हाँस (hans)—duck; नयाँ (nayan)—new ; etc.

But the dot ं (shirvindu) is used in place of ङ् , ञ् , ण् , न् or म् ; as :— बांगो—बाङ्ग (bango) curved ; संड्वों—सङ्घो (sancho)—well; अंबा—अम्बा (amba)—guava ; etc.

The 'h' sound : (visarga or dawasavindu) is used with the Sanskrit words or with the Nepali words expressing anger, contempt, irritation, etc. as :— फलतः (phalatah)—consequently, छिः (chhih) —fie ! etc.

रातो फूल	(rato phul)	—Red flower
नीलो पानी	(nilo pani)	—Blue water
सेतो ऊँट	(seti unt)	—White camel
काली बाखरी	(kali bakhri)	—Black goat.
ठूलो आमा	(thulo ama)	—Big mother
सानो बाछा	(sano bachha)	—Little calf.
नयाँ कागत	(nayan kagat)	—New paper
पुरानो कारिन्दा	(purano karinda)	—Old clerk.

LESSON—4

Conjuncts (संयुक्त-वर्ण) (Samyukt-Varna)

When two or more consonants withoou vowels they are pronounced together and are called conjuct consonants (संयुक्तबर्ण) ; as :—

क्+य=क्य   वाक्य (vakya)—sentence
द्+य=द्य   खाद्य (khadya)—food
ज्+र=ज्र   वज्र (vajra)—thunder-bolt

While pronouncing the conjuncts, it is to be noted that the first element or elements are half pronounced and the final element is fully pronounced.

The consonants may be divided into four groups for making conjucts ;

(a) Consonants ending in a vertical line; as :—ख ग च ज त न प ब म व स etc ;

The combination or the conjunct of this group of consonants is made by dropping the vertical

23

line and attaching the second consonants to the
first ;—

ग् + य = ग्य (gya)   च् + य = च्य (chya)

ज् + व = ज्व (jwa)   त् + व = त्व (twa)

न् + म = न्म (nma)   म् + म = म्म (mma)

(b) Consonants not ending in a vertical line ;
as :—ट ठ ड ढ द ह etc.

The combination with this group of consonants is formed by writing the second consonant
by the side of the first or placing the second just
below the first ; as :—

ट् + ट = ट्ट, ट्ट (tta)   ट् + ठ = ट्ठ, ट्ठ (ttha)

द् + द = द्द, द्द (dda)   द् + ध = द्ध (ddha)

ड् + ड = ड्ड, ड्ड (dda)   ह् + व = ह्व (hva)

(c) The consonants क, झ and फ

क, झ and फ in combination with other consonants,
the vertical lines are retained, but the curve on the
right is halved ; as :—

क् + ख = क्ख (kkha)

झ् + झ = झ्झ (jhjha)

फ् + त = फ्त (fta)

The vertical line and a little curve beyond is retained not to confuse half क with half व, half रू with half म and half फ with half प.

(d) The consonant र :—

When र combines with a consonant as a second one it is written as below :—

क्+र=क्र,　　　ख्+र=ख्र,　　　ग+न=ग्र, etc
कra　　　　　khra　　　　　gra

But when it combines with ट, ठ, ड, ढ, the conjuncts will be as follows :—

ट्+र=ट्र,　　　ठ्+र=ठ्र,　　　ड्+र=ड्र,　　　ढ्+र=ढ्र
tra　　　　　thra　　　　　dra　　　　　dhra

र as the first consonant assumes the form ( ) and goes over the second letter ; as :—

र+म = र्म, कर्म (karma)

र+क = र्क, तर्क (tarka)

र+ग = र्ग, दुर्गा (durga)

There are some irregular conjuncts such as :—

क्+ष=क्ष, क्ष, क्ष ksa   त्+त=त्त, त्त (tta)

ज्+पं—ज्ञ (jna, gna)   त्+र—त्र, त्र (tra)

क्+त—क्त, क्त (kta)   श्+र—श्र (sra)

ह्+म—ह्म (hma)

Read :—

मक्खन	(makhan)	butter
सिक्का	(sikka)	coin
मक्खी	(makkhi	fly
चक्का	(chakka)	wheel
नम्र	(namra)	humble
खाद्य	(khadya)	food
वाक्य	(vakya)	sentence
चक्र	(chakra)	wheel
कट्टर	(kattar)	orthodox
जुत्ता	(jutta)	shoe
सच्चा	(sachcha	true

पत्ता	(patta)	address
चश्मा	(chasma)	spectacles
चिठी	(chitthi)	letter
बिद्वान	(vidwan)	learned man
पद्म	(padma)	lotus
स्वार्थ	(swartha)	selfishness
भलाद्मी	(bhaladmi)	gentleman
भारी संदूस	(bhari sandus)	Heavy chest.
सांचो युरा	(sancho kura)	True word.
कच्चा फल	(kachcha phal)	Green fruit.
शुद्ध खादी	(sudha khadi)	Pure khaddar
सानो मन्दिर	(sano mandir	Small temple
नवाँ विद्यालय	(nayan vidyalaya)	New School
प्यारा बच्चा	(pyara bachcha)	beloved chilp·
सेतो बिरालो	(seto biralo)	White cat.
रातो जुता	(rato jutta)	Red shoe
ठूलो किताब	(thulo kitab)	Big book

LESSON—5

Pronunciation (उच्चारण)
(Uchcharan)

Every language has its own characteristic way of pro-
nuncintion of letters, It is not possible to have mastery
over it only with the help of books. So it is necessary
to use one's earnestness to have accurate knowledge in
pronounciation. The learners should take help of a
teacher and friends for this purpose. Yet efforts are to be
made to make it clear and easy as far as practicable by mere
writing.

(i) Vowels (स्वरवर्ण)
Swar-varna

अ ('a') is pronounced lik 'u' in the words
'but', 'up' etc Final अ inherent in every
consonant is usually omitted from pronunciation
(like the final 'e' in English) ; as :—

घर (ghar) house, कलम (kalam)—pen, खसम
(khasam)—husband ; etc.

आ (a) has the long sound of English 'a' in
the words 'large', 'star', 'charge' etc. as :—

आश (ash)—hope, हात (hat)—hand, काम (kam) —work ; etc.

There is no short आ in Nepali.

इ (i) has the short sound of English 'i' in 'pin', 'thin', 'him', etc. as :—दिन (din)—day, नियम (niyam)—rule, किताब (kitab)—book ; etc.

ई (i) has the long sound of English 'ee' in 'meet', 'feet', 'reel', etc. as :— वीर (vir)—hero, दीप (dip)—lamp, ईख (ikh)— feeling of revenge.

उ) u) has the short sound of English 'u' in 'put', 'pull', etc. as :—उपज (upaj) —product, दुख (dukh)—sorrow, मुरली (murali)——flute ; etc.

ऊ (u) has the long sound of English 'oo' in 'moon', 'food', 'look', etc. as :—फूल (ful) - flower, रूप (rup)—form, beauty, ऊन (un)—wool ; etc.

ऋ (ri) resembles the sound of 'ree' in English words,—street', 'free', 'creed', etc. as :— घृणा (ghrina)—hatred, तृण (trina)—straw, कृष्ण (krisna)—Krishna ; etc.

ऋ is used mostly in Sanskrit words.

ए (e) has the long sound of 'e' in the English words—'pen', hen' 'get', ete. as :—एक (ek)—one, खेल (khel)—play, पेट (pet)—belly ; etc.

ऐ (ai) –There is no similar letter in English which pronounces ऐ accurately : it is a diphthong pronounced like ai; e. g.,—ऐना (aina)—mirror, पसा (paisa)—pice, कैदी (kaidi)—prisoner ; etc.

But in Sanskrit words it is pronounced like ' oi ', as—शैल (soila) –mountain, ऐरावत (oiravat)—elephant ; etc.

ओ (O) has the long sound of ' oe ' in ' foe ', 'ow' in 'low' and 'o' in 'go' ; e. g. ओठ (oth)— lip, चोर (chor)—thief, गोल (gol)—round etc.

औ (an ao) is a diphthong and has the mixed sound of म and उ, and म and ओ ; as—कौवा

(kauva)—crow, नौलो (naulo) new, औजार
(aujar)—tools, को (kau)—blacksmith, मौसम
(masum)—season ; etc.

(ii) CONSONANTS (व्यंजनवर्ण)

(Vyanjan Varna)

A consonant (व्यंजनवर्ण) cannot be fully pronounced without the help of a vowel (स्वरवर्ण)
अ ('a') remains inherent in every consonant in
its ordinary form ; as :— क (ka)= क्+अ, (kha)
= ख्+अ, ग (ga)= ग्+अ, etc.

But when a consonant is without any vowel,
it takes a *hal* ( ) below it and is written
as :— क्, ख् ग् ; etc.

क (ka has the sound of English 'c' in 'call',
'caution' committee', etc. as :—काका (kaka)—
uncle, कलम (kalam—pen, किताब (kitab)—
book etc.

ख (kha) has the mixed sound of 'k' and 'h' as :—खेल (khel) play, खेत (khel) farm; खेलौना (khelauna) toy ; etc.

ग (ga) has the sound of 'g' in 'good', 'give' etc. as :— गाला (gala) cheek, गोल (gol) round, गुलाब (gulab) rose ; etc.

घ (gha) has the mixed sound of 'g' and 'h' as :— घर (ghar) house, घार (ghar) hive, घोड़ा horse ; etc.

ङ (n) has the nasal sound of English 'ng' in 'long', 'sing', bring' etc a s: —ङारङुर (ngarngur) squabbling, ङिच्च (ngichcha) disappointed ; etc.

च (cha) has the sound of 'ch' in English 'chalk', 'chap' 'charm'. ete. as :—चार (char) four, चमक (chamak) brightness, चाचा (chacha)

छ (chha) has the mixed sound of 'ch' and 'h' as :—छाना (chhana) roof, छाना (chhata) umbrella, अछूत (achhut) untouchable ; etc.

ण has the 'n' sound just in the same way as t and d above e. g. अणु (anu) atom, प्राण (pran,) life, गुण (gun) quality ; etc.

त (ta) has no similar sound in English. as :— तारा (tara) star, तीर (tir) arrow, तरुण (tarun) young; etc

थ (tha) has the sound of 't' and 'h' as in 'thorn' thin 'thought', etc. as : — थंपड़ी (thapadi) clapping थाह (thah) knowledge, etc.

द (da) has the sound of 'th' in 'the', 'that', then', etc. ; as : — देश (des) country , दिन (din) day, दान (dan) gift ; etc.

ध (dha) has no similar English sound. It should be pronounced like 'd' and 'h' e. g., धन (dhan) wealth, धोखा (dhoka) deception, गधा (gadha) ass; etc.

न (na) sounds like 'n' in 'not', 'narrow', nothing', etc.; as : — नदी (nadi) river, पानी (pani) water, दाना (dana) grain; etc .

प (pa) sounds like 'p' in 'paw', 'pan', 'pot' etc.; as : — पछि (pachhi) after, पिता (pita) father, पुल (pul) bridge ; etc.

फ (pha) has the sound of 'f' in 'fog', 'fall' 'food', etc ; as: –फ़ल (fal) fruit फूल (ful) flower, फसल (fasal) crop; etc.

ब (ba) sounds like 'b' in 'ball', box', 'boon'. etc. as : — बल (bal) strength, बालक (balak) boy बगली (bagali) pocket; etc.

भ (bha) has the mixed sound of 'b' and 'h' as : — भाषा (bhasa) language, भूल (bhul) mistake, भोड (bhid) crowd, etc.

म (ma) sounds like 'm' in may', 'me', 'mean', etc. as : — मन (mana) mind, माला (mala) garland, मीठो (mitho) sweet; etc.

य (ya) is pronounced like i a (इ+अ) as : — यश (yas) fame, यदि (yadi) if, यो (yo) this, यी (yi) these ; etc.

र (ra) has the sound of 'r' in 'raw', 'rat' 'rain' etc.; as : — रथ (rath) chariot, रात (rat) night, रुपैया (rupaiya) rupee etc.

ल (la) sounds like 'l' in 'lot', 'long', 'look' etc ; as : —लता (lata) creeper, लोक (lok) people, लडका (ladka) boy; etc.

व (va, wa) is pronounced like 'oa' (ओ ओ) as : —
वर (oar, war) near, वकील (o-akil, vakil wakil)
pleader; वहाँ (vahan,wahan) there; etc.

श (sa) has the sound of 'sh' in 'shop', 'ship',
'short', etc. ; as:— शरम (saram) shame, शङ्का (sanka)
doubt, शायद (sayad) perhaps, शीत (sita) dew ; etc.

ष (sa) has no similar sound in English. It is
mostly used in Sanskrit words; as : — षष्ठ (sastha)
sixth, भाषण (bhasan) speech, शेष (ses) end ; etc.

स (sa) has the souud of hissing 's' in 'saw',
'song', 'sun', etc. e g, सात (sat) seven, सलाम (salam)
salutation. सुन (sun) gold; etc.

ह (ha) sounds like 'h' in 'hot', 'hall', 'house',
etc. ; as : — हवा (hava) air, हात (hat) hand, हक (hak)
right; etc.

(m) resembles the sound of 'ng' or ,n' in
'song', 'long' 'wrong', etc ; as — अग (anga)
body, संसार (sansar) world, सारांश (sarans) substance;
etc.

: (h) visarga pronounces like a final breathing
'h' as in पुन: (punah) again, अतः (atah) then; etc.

chandra-vindu is a half-nasal sound. e. g., वहाँ (vahan) there, कहाँ (kahan) where. यहाँ (yahan) here; etc.

Words ending in simple consonants are pronounced with their म (a) silent, e. g, घर जल, कलम etc. These words are to be pronounced as घर (ghar) जल (jal) and कलम (kalam)

Practise :—

तिमी कोसग आयौ ? timi kosang ayau	With whom have you come ?
म मेरो साथी मंग आऐ ma mero sathisang ayen	I have come with my friend.
तिम्रो पिताजी को नाम के हो ? timro pita ji ko nam ke ho	What's your father's name ?
उहाँको नाम लाल बहादुर हे. uhanko nam Lal Bahadur ho	His name is Lal Bahadur.
तिम्रो नाम के हो ? timro nam ke ho	What's your name !
मेरो नाम गोपाल हो mero nam Gopal ho	My name is Gopal

यो लड्का को हो ?	
yo ladka ko ho	Who is this boy ?
यो लड्का हरिलालको भाइ हो	This boy is the younger
yo ladka Harilalko bhai ho	brother of Harilal.
कृष्ण र गोविन्द कहाँ गए ?	Where have krishna
krishna ra Govinda kahan	and Govinda
gaye	gone ?
उनीहरू विराटनगर गएका छन	They have gone to
uniharu viratnagar gayeka chhan	Biratnagar.
त्यहाँ को-को बसेका छन ?	Who are sitting there ?
tyahan ko ko baseka chhan	
त्यहाँ सीता र शकुन्तला बसेका छन	Sita and Shakuntala
tyahan sita ra shakuntala	are sitting there.
baseka chhan	

Read and write :—

हिमगिरि—मण्डित, सुगन्ध-शोभित, जय जय आमा नेपाल ।

आर्य, अनार्य-बौद्ध र हिन्दू मिश्रित हाम्रो देश विशाल ।

चीन र भारत अ कमालको

हे चिरतम बाहू-बन्धन ।

मन्दिर, गुम्बा, स्वर्गा गजूर ॥

पावनत को हे जीवन ।

डोको, टोकरी, खर्पन, खुकुरी ज्यामलहरुको मुसकान ।

कोशो, काली, कर्णालीको नित्य सरल हे कलकल गान ।

जाग्रत क्षणको माया बिम्बित उच्च कलाले चुम्बित प्राण ।

गिरि राजाको चूड़ामणि हे विश्वभरीको उज्ज्वल सान ।

अगणित हामीं नेपालीको

निर्भय यौटै बलियो ज्यान ।

English Rendering—

Victory, victory to thee, O mother Nepal,

Who is crowned with the snow-mountains

And who is fragrant and gorgeous.

Thou art our vast country composed

Of the Aryans and non-Aryans,

Buddhists and Hindus.

O eternal embracing Tie

Of China and India !

O Life of purity in the

Gold-steepled temples and gumbas !

Thou art the laughter embodied of doko,

Tokari, kharpan, khukuri and tools.

O purling song of the eternal.

Simplicity of the Koshi, Kali

And Karnali rivers !

Thou art the life kissed by
  High arts with the love of waking
    Hours reflected upon thee !
O Diamond of the highest mountains ,
  The bright Lustre of the world !
Thou art the only fortified
  And fearless Iife of us,
    The innumerable Nepalese.

━ ━ ━ ━ ━

LESSON—6

Step to Language

[भाषामा पवेश]

म   (ma) I   हामी   (hami) we
तँ   (tan) thou   तिमी   (timi) you
त्यो   (tyo) he   तिनीहरू (tiniharu) they
यो   (yo) it, this यिनीहरु (yiniharu) these
लडका   (ladka) boy   लडकी   (ladki) girl
बच्चा (bachcha) male chid बच्ची (bachchi) female
                                        child

छोरा (chhora) son   छोरी (chhori) daughter
पुत्र (putra) son   कन्या (kanya) daughter
मछु   (ma chhu)   I am
हामी छौं (hami chhaun) we are
तँ छस् (tan chhas) thou art
तिमी छौ (timi chhau) you are
त्यो छ   (tyo chha) he is
तिनीहरु छन् (tiniharu)chhan) they are

यो छ (yo chha)   this is

यिनीहरु छन् (yiniharu chhan)   these are

तपाई हुनु हुन्छ (tapain hunu hunchha)
           —you are (respectful)

म गर्छूं (ma garchhu)   I do

हामी गार्छौं (hami garchhaun)   we do

तें गर्छंस् (tan garchhas)   thou doest

तिमी गर्छौ (timi garchhau)   you do

त्यो गर्छं (tyo garchha)   he does

तिनीहरु गर्छंन् (tiniharu garchhan)   they do

तपाई हरु गनु हुन्छ (tapinharu garnu hunchha)
          —you do (respectful)

यो (yo) this   त्यो (tyo) that

यी (yi) these   ती (ti) those

यहाँ (yahan) here   बहाँ (vahan) there

जहाँ (jahan) where   कहाँ (kahan) where
                (interrogatory)

सम्म (samma) upto

यहाँ सम्म (yahan samma) upto this (place)

बहाँ सम्म (vahan samma) upto that   („)

जहाँ सम्म (Jahan samma) upto which („)

कहाँ सम्म (kahan samma) upto what („)

जस्तो (Jasto) like

यस्यो (yasto) like this   त्यस्तो (tyasto) like that
जस्तो (jasto) like that   कस्तो (kasto) like what

निम्ति (nimti) for

यसको निम्ति	(yasko nimti)	for this
उसको निम्ति	(usko nimti)	for that
त्यसको निम्ति	(tyasko nimti	for that
के को निम्ति	(ke ko nimti)	for what

लागि (lagi) for

यसको लागि	(yasko lagi)	for this
त्यसको लागि	(tyasko lagi)	for that
उसको लागि	(usko lagi)	for that
के को लागि	(ke ko lagi)	for what

ठूलो	(thulo)	big	सानो	(sano)	small
नयाँ	(nayan)	new	पुरानो	(purano)	old
असल	(asal)	good	खराब	(kharab)	bad
भित्र	(bhitra)	in	बाहिर	(bahira)	out
कि	(ki)	that	को	(ko)	who
केही	(kehi)	a few	कोही	(kohi)	some body

किन (kina) why   किन भने (kina bhane) because

जसै (jasai) as   उसै (usai) so like

यदि (yadi) if   तर (tara) but

उसमाथि (usmathi) besides   किन्तु (kintu) but

परन्तु (parantu) but   उसमा पनि (usma pani) more over

हुन्छ (hunchha) all right   त्यस्तो हो भने (tyasto ho bhane) if so

वा (va) or   र (ra) and

फेरि (pheri) again   पनि (pani) also

धेर (dherai) more   थोरै (thorai) a little

यति (yati) this much   उति (uti) that much

जति (jati) as much   कति (kati) how much

अब (ab) now   तब (tab) then

जब (jab) when   कहिले (kahile) when interrogatory

Names of the directions (दिशाहरूको नाम)

पूर्व (purva) East

पचिम (paschim) West

उत्तर (uttar) North

दक्षिए (daksin) South

दायाँ (dayan) Right

बायाँ (bayan) Left

Names of the days (दिनहरूको नाम)

सोमवार	(somvar)	Monday
मंगलवार	(mangalvar)	Tuesday
बुधवार	(budhvar)	Wednesday
ब्रृहस्पतिवार	(brihaspativar)	Thursday
शुक्रवार	(sukravar)	Friday
शनिवार	(sanivar)	Saturday
शनिचरवार	(sanischarvar)	Saturday
रविवार	(ravivar)	Sunday
आइतवार	(aitwar)	Sunday

Read and write:—

नयाँ कपड़ा	(nayan kapada)	new cloth
पुरानो जुत्ता	(purano jutta)	old shoe
केरै भात	(dherai bhat)	much rice

थोरै दाल	(thorai dal)	a little pulse
ठूलो लड्का	(thulo ladka)	a grown up boy
सानी लड्की	(sani ladki)	a little girl
कति असल	(kati asal)	how good
जाति राम्रो	(jati ramro)	as beautiful as
कस्तो देश	(kasto desh)	what sort of country
यस्तो होइन	(yasto hoina)	not like this
कांचो आँप	(kancho anp)	unripe mango
पक्का मानिस	(pakka manis)	righteous man
मीठो बोली	(mitho boli)	sweet word
शद्ध प्रेम	(suddha prem)	pure love

कृष्ण असल लड्का हो
Krishan asal ladka ho

Krishan is a good boy

सीता खराब लड्की हुन्
Sita kharab ladki hun

Sita is a bad girl.

तिमी कहाँ जान लागेका छौ ?
timi kahan jana lageka chhaun

Where are you going

हामी बाहिर जान लागेका छौं
hami bahira jana lageka chhaun

We are going out .

उनीहरू कहिले आउछन्   When will they come
uniharu kahile aunchhan

उनीहरू सोमवार आउछन्   They will come on
uniharu somvar aunchhan Monday.

Exercise

Translate into Nepali :—

I, he, they, boy, girl, here, there, north, south,
hour, month, how, now, when, in, out, if, this, that.

LESSON—7

NUMBER—गन्ति (Ganti)

१	२	३	४	५	६	७
एक	दुह	तीन	चार	पांच	छः	सात
८	९	१०	११	१२	१३	१४
आठ	नौ	दश	एधार	बाह	तेह	चौध
१५	१६	१७	१८	१९	२०	२१
पन्ध	सोह	सत्र	अठाह	उन्नैंस	बीस	एक्काइस
२२	२३	२४	२५	२६	२७	२८
बाइस	तेइस	चौबीस	पचीस	छब्बीस	सत्तइस	अठाइस
२९	३०	३१	३२	३३	३४	३५
उनन्तीस	तीस	एकतीस	बत्तीस	तेतीस	चौंतीस	पत्तीस
३६	३७	३८	३९	४०	४१	४२
छतीस	सैंतीस	अठतीस	उनन्चालीस	चालीस	एकचालीस	बयालीस
४३	४४	४५	४६	४७	४८	४९
त्रियालीस	चवालीस	पेंतालीस	छयालीस	सतचालीस	अठचालीस	उनन्चास
५०	५१	५२	५३	५४	५५	५६
पचास	एकाउन	बाउन	त्रिपन	चवन	पचपन	छपन

५७	५८	५९	६०	६१	६२	६३
सन्ताउन	अन्ठाउन	उन्साठी	साठी	एकसाट्ठी	बयासट्ठी	त्रिसट्ठी

६४	६५	६६	६७	६८	६९	७०
चौंसट्ठी	पैंसट्ठी	छंसट्ठी	सत्सट्ठी	अठसट्ठी	उगहत्तर	सतरी

७१	७५	७३	७४	७५	७६	७७
एकत्तहर	वहत्तर	त्रिहत्तर	चौहत्तर	पचहत्तर	छंहत्तर	सतहत्तर

७८	७९	८०	८१	८२	८३	८४
अठहत्तर	उनासी	असी	एकासी	बयासीं	त्रियासी	चौरासी

८५	८६	८७	८८	८९	९०	९१
पचासी	छयासी	सतासी	अठासी	उनानब्बे	नब्बे	एकानब्बे

९२	९३	९४	९५	९६	९७	९८
बयानब्बे	त्रियानब्बे	चौरानब्बे	पचानब्बे	छयानब्बे	सन्तानब्बे	अठानब्बे

९९	१००
उनान्सय	सय

२००	३००	४००	५००
दुह सय	तीन सय	चार सय	पाँच सय

१०००	१००००	१०००००	१००००००
हजार	दश हजार	लाख	करोड़

NUMBER

ordinals (क्रमसंख्या)

(Krama-sankhya)

पहिलो	(pahilo)	first
दोश्रो	(dosro)	second
तेश्रो	(tesro)	third
चौथो	(chautho)	fourth
पाँचौं	(panchaun)	fifth
छेठौं	(chhaithaun)	sixth
सातौं	(sataun)	seventh
आठौं	(athaun)	eighth
नवौं	(navaun)	ninth
दशौं	(dashaun)	tenth

To make the ordinal numbers 'औं' should be added to the remaining cardinals; as:—

एवारौं	(egharaun)	eleven ;
सोहौं	(sorhaun)	sixteenth ;
बीसौं	(bisaun)	twentieth ;
सयौं	(sayaun)	hundredth, etc.

Practise :—

एक मानिस	(ek manis)	
एउटा मानिस	(euta manis)	
एकजना मानिस	(ekjana manis)	one man
पहिलो मानिस	(pahilo manis)—the first man	
दुइ लड्का	(dui ladka)	
दुइटा लड्का	(duita ladka)	
दुइजना लड्का	(duijana ladka)	two boys
दोश्रो लड्का	(dosro ladka)—the second boy	
तीन लड्की	(tin ladki)	
तीनवटी लड्की	(tinwati ladki)	
तीनजना लड्की	(tinjana ladki)	three girls
तेश्रो लड्की	(tesro ladki)—the third girl	
चार फल	(char phal)	
चारवटा फल	(charwata phal)	four fruit
चौथो फल	(chautho phal)—the four fruit	
पांच पुस्तक	(panch pustak)	
पांचबटा पुस्तक	(panchwata pustak)	five books
पांचौं पुस्तक	(panchaun pustak)—the fifth book	

अलाई एक किताब देऊ

malai ek kitab deu

Give me a book.

सीता को लागि दुइटा ग्रांपर दुइटा केरा ल्याऊ

Sita ko lagi duita anp ra duita kera lyau

Bring two mangoes and two bananas for Sita.

यस पाठशालामा पाचसय लड्की पढ्छन्

yas pathsalama panchsaya ladki padhchhan

Five hundred Girls read in this school.

पहिलो र चौथो लड्का

pahilo ra chautho ladka

The first and the fourth boy.

पहिलो दर्जाको दोश्रो लड्की

pahilo darjako dosro ladki

The second girl of the first class.

Exercise

Translate into Nepali :—

5 6, 9, 11, 18, 29, 37, 88, 99, thirteen, nineteen,
thirtyone, seventysix, eightynine , fourth, sixth,
ninth, tenth, twelfth, nineteenth, twentieth.

LESSON 8

Noun, Adjective & Pronoun (नाम, विशेशण र सर्वेनाम)

Noun (नाम)

Nouns are of five kinds as :—

    (a)   **Proper noun** (व्यक्तिवाचक नाम) is the name of a particular person, place or thing. e. g. बुद्ध (Buddha), वीरगञ्ज (Birganj), विरात्नगर (Biratnagar); श्याम (Shyam), हरी (Hari) etc.

    (b)   **Common noun** (जातिवाचक नाम) is the name of everything of the same class or kind. e. g. किताब (book), बिरालो (cat), लड्की (girl), फल (fruit), रूख (tree); लड्का (boy), पशु (beast) etc.

    (c)   **Collective noun** (समुदयवाचक नाम) is the name given to a number of persons, animals or things classified as a whole. e. g. श्रेणी (class), सेना (army), भीड (crowd) ; etc.

    (d)   **Material noun** (द्रव्यवाचक नाम) specifies what a thing is made of. e. g. पानी (water), चांदी (silver); सुन (gold), फलाम (iron), etc.

(e)   **Abstract noun** (भाववाचक नाम) is the name of a quality state or action. e. g. सुख (weal), दुःख (woe) दौड (race). जवानी (youth) ; etc.

Abstract noun is formed in three different ways, as:—

(1)   from nouns :—

मित्र + ता = मित्रता	friendship
चोर + ई = चोरी	theft
अमीर + पना = अमीरपना	nobility
चाकर + ई = चाकरी	servility

(2)   from adjectives :—

सुन्दर + ता = सुन्दरता	beauty
ऊँचा + ई = ऊँचाई	height
लामो + ई = लमाई	length
दुष्ट + आई = दुष्टाई	wickedness

(3)   from verbs :—

हिड् + नु = हिड नु	walking
भन् + आउ = भनाउ	saying

पढ़ + आइ = पढाइ   reading

दौड + अ = दौड   race

There are four kinds of adjectives

(1) Qualitative Adjective (गुणबोधक विशेषण)

(2) Quantitative Adjective (परिमाणबोधक विशेषण)

(3) Numeral Adjective (संख्याबोधक विशेषण)

(4) Pronominal Adjective (सार्वनामिक विशेषण)

(1) **Qualitative Adjective** (गुणबोधक विशेषण) **means an** adjective which qualifies a thing or a person etc. as :—

असल लड्का	(asal ladka)	good boy
राम्रो लड्की	(ramri ladki)	beautiful girl
नीलो पानीं	(nilo pani)	blue water
रातो फूल	(rato phul)	red flower
कालो बाख्री	(kalo bakhri)	black goat
खराब कारिन्दा	(kharab karinda)	bad clerk
भद्दा लुगा	(bhadda luga)	indecent dress

There are two kinds of Adjectives

(i) Common (सामान्य) :—

जान्ने	(janne)	expert
राम्रो	(ramro)	beautiful
पढेको	(padheko)	educated

(ii) Proper (विशेष) :—

डोटयाल बोली (dotyal boli) Dialect spoken at Doti:

भादगाउँले टोपी (bhadgaunle topi) A cap made at Bhaktapur.

जुम्लो काम्लो (jumli kamlo) blanket made in Jumla district.

पाल्पाली भांडा (palpali bhanda) A pot made at palpa

(2) Quantitative Adjective (परिमाणबोधक विशेषण)

which refers to some quantity or measure of something ; as :—

आधा घंटा (adha ghanta) half an hour

थोरै पानी (thorai pani) a little water

पाँच गज कपडा (panch gaj kapada) five yards of cloth

तमाम दुनियाँ (tamam duniyan) the entire world

धेरै खाना (dherai khana) much food

(3) Numeral Adjective (संख्याबोधक विशेषण)

which denotes tne numder of a person or thing, etc. as :—

पहिलो मानिस (pahilo manis) the first man

एक पुस्तक (ek pustak) one book

दुइजना मानिस (duijana manis) two men

तीनवटा घोडा (tinwata ghoda) three horses

चारजना बालक (charjana balak) four boys

चौथो कोठा (chautho kotha) the fourtn room

(4) Pronominal Adjective (सार्वनामिक बिशेषण)

which in the form of a Pronoun, is used to qualify a thing or a person ; as :—

यो किताब	(yo kitab)	this book
कुन घर	(kun ghar)	which house
त्यो मानिस	(tyo manis)	that man

Pronominal Adjectives are of three kinds :—

(i) Demonstrative (दर्शक)

त्यो (tyo) that यो (yo) this उ (u) that

(ii) Relative (सम्बन्धी) :—

जो (jo) who जुन (jun) which

(iii) Interrogative (प्रश्नार्थक) :—

को (ko) who   कुन (kun) which

Pronominal Adjectives change their forms according to the number as follows :—

Singular		Plural	
त्यो (tyo)			
सो (so)	that	ती (ti)	those
त्यस (tyasa)			
यो (yo)			
यस (yasa)	this	यी (yi)	these
उ (u)			
उस (usa)	that	ऊ (u)	those
जो (jo)	who	जो (jo)	who
जुन (jun)	which		which
जस (jasa)	what	जुन (jun)	whose
	that		
को (ko)	who		who
कुन (kun)	which	को (ko)	which
कस (kasa)	what	कुन (kun)	what
	that		those

Other kinds of Adjectives change their forms as follows :—

(i) Adjectives ending in ओ make their plural forms by changing the final ओं into आ ; as :—

Singular	Plural
कालो कोट (kalo kot)	काला कोट (kala kot)
a black coat	black coats
ठूलो मानिस (thulo manis)	ठूला मानिस (thula manis)
a great man	great men
गोरो छोरो (goro chhoro)	गोरा छोरा (gora chhora)
a white son	white sons

(ii) All adjectives ending in ओ and some in आ as हा, वा, टा take their feminine forms (singular and in the sense of honour only) by changing them into ई ; as :—

कालो केटो (kalo keto)	काली केटी (kali keti)
a black boy	a black girl
बहुलाहा युवक (bahulaha yuvak)	बहुलाही युवती (bahulahi yuvati)
a mad young man	a mad young girl
एउटा मानिस (eute mains)	एउटी स्वास्नी मानिस (euti swasni manis)
one man	one woman
खञ्चुवा (khanchuwa)	खञ्चुवी (khanchuwi)
fond of eating (male)	fond of eating (female)

But while denoting honour in the case of masculine nouns, and while making their plural forms in the case of the nouns of all the genders, they change their endings into श्रा, not ई; as :—

एउटा, सानो, राम्रो केटो छ   There is a little,
(euta, sano, ramro keto chha)   beautiful boy,

दुइटा, राम्रा, साना केटाहरू   There are two beautiful
श्रथवा केटीहरू छन् (duita ramra,   little boys or girls.
sana ketaharu athava
ketiharu chhan

(iii) Qualitative Adjectives referring to human beings and ending in श्र, या, ई or ए make their feminine forms by changing the final श्र, या, ई or ए into इनी, एनी, नी or यी; as :—

Masculine	*Feminine*
चतुर (chatur) clever	चतुर्नी (chaturni)
सहरिया (sahariya) town-dweller	सहरिनी (saharini)
श्रभागी (abhagi) ill-fated man	श्रभागिनी (abhagini)
पाखे (pakhe) rough	पखिनी (pakhini)

Adjectives other than the above and ending in श्र (हल्) etc. do not change their forms; as :—

दुइ (dui) two   मानिस (manis) man
बेस (bes) good   मानिसहरु (manisharu) men

असल (asal) good

खराब (kharab) bad स्त्री (stri) woman

चार (char) four स्त्रीहरू (striharu) women

साधा (sadha) simple

जाती (jati) good काम (kam) work

सज्जन (sajjan) कामहरू (kamharu) works

An Adjective can also be used as a Noun; as :—

बूढालाई मद्दत गर (budhalai maddat gar)— Help the old man.

सबै आए (sabai aye)— All came.

चारबटीलाई बोलाउ (charwatilai bolau)— Call the four women.

Comparison of Adjectives

There are three degrees of comparison : (i) Positive, (ii) Comparitive, (iii) Superlative.

(i) Positive :—

यो फूल राम्रो छ
yo phul ramro chha

This flower is beautiful.

यो लडका असल छ
yo ladka asal chha

This boy is good.

त्यो कपड़ा मसीनो छ
tyo kapada masino chha

That cloth is fine

(ii) Comparative :—

यो फूल त्यो फूलभन्दा राम्रो छ
yo phul tyo phulbhanda
ramro chha

This flower is more beautiful than that flower.

यो लड्का त्यो लड्काभन्दा असल छ
yo ladka tyo ladka
bhanda asal chha

This boy is better than that boy.

यो कपडा भन्दा मसीनो छ
yo kapada tyo kapada
bhanda masino chha

This cloth is finer than that cloth.

(iii) Superlative :—

यो फूल सबभन्दा राम्रो छ
yo phul sabaibhanda
ramro chna

Thia flower is the most beautiful of all.

यो लड्का सबैभन्दा असल छ
yo ladka sabaibhanda
asal chha

This boy is the best of all.

यो कपडा सबैभन्दा मसीनो छ
yo kapada sabaibhanda
masino chha

This cloth is the finest of all.

Pronouns (सर्वनाम)

A pronoun used in place of a noun. Its number and gender are formed according to the noun. There are twelve pronouns in Nepali, such as:— म, तैं, त्यो, यो, उ, तपाई, यहाँ, त्यहाँ, उहाँ, आफू, जो and को ।

Pronouns are divided into five classes :—

(1) : Personal (पुरुषवाचक), (2) Demonstrative (दर्शक) (3) Relative (सम्बन्धवाचक) , (4) Interrogative (प्रश्नबाचक), (5) Definite and Indefinite (निश्चय तथा अनिश्चबाचक).

(i) Personal Pronouns stand for persons. They are of five kinds ; as :—

(a) First

म (ma) I	हामी (hami)
	हामीहरू (hamiharu) we

(b) Second

तैं (tan) thou	तिमी (timi)
	तिमीहरु (timiharu) you

(c) Third —

त्यो (tyo) he	
तिनी (tini) shi	तिनीहरू (tiniharu) they
यो (yo) it	

(d) Honorific :—

तपाई (tapain) you	तपाईहरू (tapainharu) you
उहाँ (uhan) he	उहाँहरू (uhanharu) they

(e) Reflexive :—

म आफै जाउँला

ma aphai jaunla   I shall go myself.

तिमी स्वयं गन सक्छौं   You can do yourself.

timi swayam garna sakchhau

(2) Demonstrative Pronouns demonstrate some particular thing near or far ; such as :—

यो (yo) this   यी (ye) these

त्यो (tyo) that   ती (ti) those

यो मेरो हात हो   This is my hand.

yo mero hat ho

त्यो रामको घर हो   That is Ram's house.

tyo Ramko ghar ho

यी आँप हुन्   These are mangoes.

yi anp hun

ती गुलाब हुन्   Those are roses.

ti gulab hun

(3) Relative Pronouns not only refer to a noun or noun-equivalent, but also join two sentences together.

जो (jo) who   जे (je) what

जुन (jun) which

जो जान्छ त्यसले पाउँछ
jo janchha tyasle
paunchha

He, who goes, gets.

मोहन ! जो तिम्रो साथी हौ,
त्यो मेरो स्कूलसा पढ्छ
Mohan ! jo timro sathi
ho, tyo mero schoolma
padhchha

Mohan ! he, who is
your friend, reads in my
school.

त्यो कलम जुन रातो छ मेरो हो
tyo kalam jun rato chha
mero ho

The pen, which is red,
is mine.

(4) Interrogative Pronouns ask questions ; as :—

को जान्छ ?
ko janchha

Who goes ?

यो के हो ?
yo ke ho

What is this ?

तिम्रो किताब कुनचाहीं हो ?
timro kitab kunchahin ho

Which is your book ?

तिमी के गर्न चाहन्छौ ?
timi ke garna chahanchhau

What do you want
to do ?

(5) Definite and Indefinite :—

यो (yo) this   त्यो (tyo) that
केही (kehi) something कोही (kohi) somebody

जेसुकै (jesukai) anything   जोसुकै (josukai) anybody

म यो जान्दिन   I do not know this

ma yo jandin

त्यो उसले पायो   He got that.

tyo usale payo

केही त खान सक्नु हुन्छ   You may take some-

kehi ta khan saknu   thing at least.

huncha

जो सुकै जान सक्छ   Anybody can go.

jo sukai jana sakchha

Revision Lesson

Pronouns are divided into five classes :—

(1) Personal :—

म (I), तँ (thou), त्यो (he), तिनी (she), यो (it), हामी (we), तिमी (you), तपाई (you— respectful), तिनीहरु (they).

(2) Reflexive :—

आफू स्वयं (self)

(3) Relative :—

जो (who), जुन (which), जे (what)

(4) **Interrogative** :—

को (who), कुन (which), के (what)

(5) **Definite and Indefinite** :—

यो (this)   केही (something)

त्यो (that)   कोही (somebody)

जेसुकै (anything)   जोसुकै (anybody)

N.B.—आफै can be used both as a personal and a rflexive pronoun ; as :—

तिमि कहाँ जाने हो ? timi kahan jane ho	Where are you going ?
म आफै जाउँला ma aphai jaunla	I shall go myself.
तिमी आफै किन गर्दैनौं timi aphai kina gardainaun	Why do you not do it yourself ?

Exercise

1. How many kinds of pronouns are there in Nepali ! Cive two examples

2. Pick up the pronouns from the following sentences and say what kinds of pronouns are they :

यो को हो ? म आफै गर्नं चाहन्छु । के हेरिरहे छौ ? केही त लेऊ । जो आएको थियो त्यो राती नै गयो । जोसुकै जान सक्छ । के हेछौं ? यो के हो ?

LESSON—9

verb—क्रियापद (kriyapad)

A verb is a word which says something about some person or thing; as —खान्छु, जान्छ, बस्ला etc.

In Nepali verbs are formed according to the number, gender and person of the nominative. As for example :—

लड्का जान्छ (ladka janchha)	The boy goes.
उड्की जान्छिन् (ladki janchhin)	The girl goes.
म गर्छु (ma garchhu)	I do.
तिनीहरू गछन् (tiniharu garchhn)	They do.

Verbs are generally of two kinds :—(1) Transitive (सकर्मक) and (2) Intransitive (अकर्मक).

(i) A Transitive verb denotes an action the effect of which passes on to an object; as:—

त्यो फल खान्छ (tyo phal khanchha)—**He eats a fruit.**

Here खान्छ is a transitive verb, because it requires the object फल to complete its sense.

(ii) An Intransitive verb has no object ; i
completes the sense itself ; as :—

त्यो जान्छ (tyo janchha) He goes.

त्यो दगुछं (tyo dagurcha) He runs.

The verb in Nepali has four chief parts :

(a) The infinitive, (b) the root, (c) the
present (or imperfect) participle and (d) the
past (perfect) participle.

(a) The infinitive is the original form of
the verb always ending in as :—

गर्नु (to do), जान्नु (to know), लेख्नु (to write),
पढ्नु (to read) etc.

(d) The root is obtained by cutting off the
'नु' from the infinitive ; as :—गर्न—गर्, जान्नु—जान्,
लेख्नु—लेख्, पढ्नु —पढ् etc.

(c) The present or the imperfect participle
is formed by adding दो to the root ; as :-- गर्दों,
जान्दो, लेख्दो, पढ्दो etc.

(d) The past or the perfect participle is
formed by adding एको to the root ; as :—गरेको,
यानेको, लेखेको पढेको etc.

Some present and past participles are formed irregularly ; as :—

जानु (to go) { जाँदो / गएको

हुनु (to be) { हुँदो / भएको

धुनु (to wash) { धुँदो / धोएको

A list of some transitive and intransitive verbs is given below :—

Intransitive			Transitive		
आउनु	—	to come	गर्नु	—	to do
उठनु	—	to rise	भन्नु	—	to tell
उखनु	—	to jump	काट्नु	—	to cut
खस्नु	—	to fall	किन्नु	—	to buy
चढ्नु	—	to climb	खानु	—	to eat
चल्नु	—	to move	जान्नु	—	to know
जानु	—	to go	देख्नु	—	to see
डराउनु	—	to fear	दिनु	—	to give
पौडनु	—	to swim	धुनु	—	to wash

दौडनु	— to run	नाप्नु	— to measure
नाच्नु	— to dance	पढनु	— to read
पुग्नु	— to reach	पिउनु	— to drink
बच्नु	— to live	सोध्नु	— to ask
भुण्डिनु	— to hang	बेच्नु	— to sell
मर्नु	— to die	राख्नु	— to keep
रहनु	— to stay	लादनु	— to load
लाग्नु	— to stick	लिनु	— to take
सुत्नु	— to sleep	सम्भनु	— to understand
हाँस्नु	— to laugh	सिउनु	— to sew
हुनु	— to be	सुन्नु	— to hear

Verbs are divided into two other groups Complete and Incomplete.

Complete verbs denote a complete sense of something done ; as :—देख्छ (sees), गछ (does), आयो (came), गयो (went) etc.

Incomplete verbs denote an incomplete sense of something done ; as :—देखेर (seeing), सुनेर (hearing), आएर (coming). गएर (going) etc.

Causative Verb (प्रेरणार्थंक क्रिया)

There are two forms of causative verbs in Nepali.

The first form of causative verbs is formed by adding ग्राउ, याउ, वाउ or लाउ before the नु of the infinitive ; as :—

पढनु (to read) पढाउनु (to make read)

उभिनु (to stand) उभ्याउनु (to make stand)

छुनु (to touch) छुवाउनु (to make touch)

दिनु (to give) दिलाउनु (to make give)

The second form of causative verbs is formed by adding लाउनु after the infinitive of the first form of the causative verbs. In that case the नु of the infinitive is changed into न ; as :—

पढाउनु (to get read)—पढाउन लाउनु (to tell another person to get it read by a third man)

लेखाउनु (to get written)—लेखाउन लाउनु (to tell another person to get it written by a third man).

Examples

म रूख चढ्छु—I climb up a tree.

म उसलाई रूख चढाउँछु—I make him climb up a tree.

म उसलाई रुख चढांउन लाउछु—I make him (by some person) climb up a tree.

म तसंन्छु—I fear.

म उसलाई तर्साउँछु—I frighten him.

म उसलाई तर्साउन लाउँछु—I get him frightened by some person.

म हाँस्छु—I laugh,

म उसलाई हँसाउँछु—I make him laugh.

म उसलाई हँसाउन लाउँछु—I make him laugh by some person

म सुत्छु—I sleep.

म उसलाई सुराउँछु—I make him fall asleep,

म उसलाई सुताउन लाउँछु—I make him fall asleep by some person.

A list of some Intransitive Verbs showing their transitive and causative forms :—

Intransitive	Transitive	Causative
मर्नु (die)	मार्नु	मराउनु
चल्नु (move)	चाल्नु	चलाउनु
झर्नु (fall)	झार्नु	झराउनु
तर्नु (cross)	तार्नु	तराउनु
बल्नु (burn)	बाल्नु	बलाउनु
गल्नु (melt)	गाल्नु	गलाउनु

A list of some transitive verbs with their more than one causative forms :—

Tran. verb	First cau. form	Sec. cau. form	Third cau. form
दिन (to give)	दिग्राउन	दियाउन	दिलाउन

छुनु (to touch)	छुम्राउनु	छुवाउनु	छुलाउनु
पिउनु (to drink)	पिम्राउनु	पियाउनु	पिलाउनु
सिउनु (to sew)	सिम्राउनु	सियाउनु	सिलाउनु
रुनु (to weep)	रुम्राउनु	रुवाउनु	रुलाउनु
जिउनु (to live)	जिम्राउनु	जियाउनु	जिलाउनु
धुनु (to wash)	धुम्राउनु	ध्वाउनु	धुलाउनु

Exercise

1. What are the differences between transitive and intransitive verbs ? Give two examples.

2. What is an incomplete verb ? Give to examples.

3. Pick up the transitive and intransitive verbs from the following words and transform them into transitive forms :

खस्नु, बोल्नु, चढ्नु, हाँस्नु, देख्नु, लेट्नु, रुनु, उठ्नु, सुत्नु, जिउनु, खानु, मनु ।

———

LESSON—10

Gender— लिग (ling)

Gender (लिग) is the difference of sex. There are altogether four genders in Nepali—Masculine (पुंलिङ्ग), Feminine (स्त्रीलिङ्ग), Neuter (नपुंसकलिङ्ग) and Common (सामान्यलिङ्ग)

Names of males are always masculine ; as ; बाबु (babu) father, राजा (raja) king, छोरा (chhora) son, घोडा (ghoda) horse गोपाल (Gopal) Gopal, etc.

Names of females are always feminine ; as : आमा (ama) mother, रानी (rani) queen, छोरी (chhori) daughter, घोडी (ghodi) mare, etc.

Almost all things other than male or female are neuter ; as :—घर (ghar) house, पुस्तक (pustak) book, रूख (rukh) tree, फूल (phul) flower, सहर (sahar) town etc.

Names denoting animals of either sex are common ; as :— चरा (chara) bird, कीरा (kira) worm, जनावर (janawar) animal, दोपाया (dopaya) biped, देवता (devata) deity, कवि (kavi) poet etc.

74

There are three different ways by which a Masculine noun is distinguished from a Feminine :

(i) By a change of word ; as :—

Masculine	Feminine
माले (male)	पोथी (female)
दाज्यू (elder brother)	भाउज्यू (elder brother's wife)
लोग्ने (husband)	स्वास्नी (wife)
बाबु (father)	ग्रामा (mother)
भाइ (younger brother)	बुहारी (brother's wife)
मता (male elephant)	ढाई (female elephant)
ससुरा (father-in-law	सासु (mother-in-law)
मामा (maternal uncle)	माइज्यू (maternal aunt)
भ्रांक (stag)	मुड्ली (hind)

(ii) By adding a word ; as :—

Masculine	Feminine
लोग्नेमानिस (man)	स्वास्नोमानिस (woman)
पुरुष देवता (god)	स्त्री देवता (goddess)
भाले कमिला (he-ant)	पोथी कमिला (she ant)

(iii) By adding इनी, एनी, ई, नीं, ग्रानी etc. as :—

Masculine	Feminine
बिष्ट (a man of the Bishta family)	विष्टिनी (a woman of the Bishta family)

Masculine	Feminine
सुब्बा (a man of the rank of Subha)	सुब्बिना (a woman of the rank of Subha)
कुमाले (potter)	कुमालेनी (potteress)
काका (uncle)	काकीं (aunt)
केटो (boy)	केटी (girl)
नाति (grand son)	नातिनी (grand daughter)
माली (male gardener	मालिनी (female gardener)
साहू (male merchant)	साहुनी (female merchant)
कौ (he-blacksmith)	कोनी (she-blacksmith)
बाघ (tiger)	बघिनी (tigress)
देवर (brother in law)	देवरानी (sister-in-law)

The following modes of distinction between Masculine and Feminine are exceptional :—

Masculine	Feminine
गुरु (teacher)	गुरुमा (teacheress)
राजा (king)	रानी (queen)
महाराज (king)	महारानी (queen)
चोर (male thief)	चोनीं (female thief)
राज्ये (grand father)	बज्यै (grand mother)

Foreign names are classified according to the sex they denote in Nepali ; as ;

Sanskrit :—

Masc.	पति (husband)	मित्र (friend)
Fem.	पत्नी (wife)	कुमारी (virgin)
Neuter	इच्छा (wish)	धन (wealth)

English :—

Masc.	जर्नेल (General)	
Fem.	लेडी (Lady)	
Neuter	इन्जन (engine)	कोट (coat)

Urdu :—

Masc.	नवाब (Nawab)
Fem.	बेगम (Begum)
Neuter	ज्यान (life)

It is not therefore difficult to ascertain genders of a word in Nepali. Genders are known by means of objects which they denote.

Examples

असल असल किताब ल्याऊ—asal asal kitab lyau
Bring good books.

चरा गाउछ—chara gauncha
The bird sings.

भूठो कुरा किन गर्छौं ? jhutho kura kina garchhau
Why do you tell a lie. ?

लडका पाठशाला जान्छ—ladka pathsala janchha
The boy goes to school.

तिम्रो कुरा सांचो होइन – timro kura sancho hoina
Your word is not true.

लडकी घर श्राउछिन—ladki ghar aunchhin
The girl comes home.

पानी घेरै चीसो छ—pani dherai chiso chha
The water is very cold.

दुवै श्रामा बाबुको इज्जत गछ्न—dubai ama babuko ijjat
garchhan
Both of them respect their parents.

कैदीलाई ठूलो सजायं भयो—kaidilai thulo sajayan bhayo
The prisoner was punished severely.

खराब बानी छोड— kharab bani chhod
Give up your bad habit.

गहिरो नदीको पानीमा नुहाऊ—gahiro nadiko panima
nuhau
Bathe in the water of a deep river.

सोहन पक्का मानिस हो—sohan pakka manis ho
Sohan is an upright man.

मेरो बाबु धेरै दयालु हुनुहुन्छ—mero babu dherai dayalu hunuhunchha

My father is very kind.

मेरो भाइ राम्रो छ—mero bhai ramro chha

My brother is good.

तिम्री छोरी कहां गई—timri chhori kahan gai

Where has your daughter gone ?

मेरी आमा धेरै जाती हुनुहुन्छ – meri ama dherai jati hunu hunchha

My mother is very good.

Exercise

Change the gender of :—

राजा, गुरुमा, मूर्ति, किताब, कुकुर, भाइ, माछा, दिन, भाउज्यू, कुमाले ।

LESSON—11

Number—वचन (vachan)

There are two numbers : Singular (एकवचन) and Plural (बहुवचन).

Plural forms are generally made by adding हरू (haru) with the noun ; as :—

Singular	Plural
गाई (a cow)	गाईहरू (cows)
खेत (a farm)	खेतहरू (farms)
मुनि (a sage)	मुनिहरू (sages)
टोपी (a cap)	टोपीहरू (caps)
साधु (a hermit)	साधुहरू (hermits)
फल (a fruit)	फलहरू (fruits)

They can also be made without adding हरू. In that case the number of the noun is known through the verb ; as :—

Plural

मानिस मरे (manis mare) – Men died.
रूख ढले (Rukh dhale)—Trees fell.

Singular

मानिस मर्‍यो (manis maryo)—A men died.

रूख ढल्यो (Rukh dhalyo)—A tree fell.

Nouns change their forms according to numbers :—

(a) Singular nouns ending in 'ओ' change into 'आ' ; as :—

Singular	Plural
भ्यागुतो (bhyaguto) frog	भ्यागुताहरू, भ्यागुता (bhyaguta-haru, bhyaguta) frogs.
पाठो (patho) lamb	पाठाहरू, पाठा (pathaharu, patha) lambs.
भांडो (bhando) pot	भांडाहरू, भांडा (bhandaharu bhanda) pots.
छोरो (chhoro) son	छोराहरू, छोरा (chhoraharu, chhora) sons.

(b) Singular nouns ending in 'नु' change into 'ना' in plural numbers ; as :—

Singular	Plural
दुनु (dunu) leaf-pot	दुनाहरू, दुना (dunaharu, duna) leaf-pots
छानु (chhanu) roof	छानाहरू, छाना (chhanaharu, chhana) roofs

मानु (manu) a vessel   मानाहरू, माना (manaharu,
(containing 1/7 gallon)   mana) vessels

Exception : – Sanskrit nouns ending in 'नु' do
not change into 'ना' in plural number ; as :—

Singular   Plural

धनु (dhanu) bow   धनु, धनुहरू (dhanu, dhanu-
                                        haru (bows)

Honorific Plural

Singular nouns in honorific sense take plural
forms. They are not, however, added with हरू
(haru) ; as :—

कृष्ण को छोरा आयो (Krishanko chhora ayo)—Krishan
                                           son came.
भाइले पाठ पढयो (bhaile path padhyo)—My brother
                                    reads his lesson.

The same is the case with the Pronouns.
Pronouns used in the honorific sense take plural
forms only ; as :—

तेसले भन्छ (tesley bhanchha) – He says.

तिमी जान्छौ (timi janchhau)—You go.

तिनी पढ् छिन् (tini padhchhin)—She reads.

हरू (haru)

The suffix हरू is used sometimes in the sense of 'etc.', and 'others' ; as :—

रामहरू गए (Ramharu gaye)—Ram and other persons went.

सुनहरूकिनें (sunharu kinen)—I bought gold, silver etc.

गाईहरू मरे (gaiharu mare)—Cows, buffaloes etc. died.

छोराहरू सुते (chhoraharu sute)—Sons and daughters slept.

Sometimes the suffix गण is also added to the nouns for their plural forms ; as :—

ब्राह्मणगण — Brahmins

लेखकगण — writers

Examples

छानु भत्कन्छ —chhanu bhatkanchha
A roof falls,

छाना भत्कन्छन्—chhana bhatkanchhan
Roofs fall

एउटा पाठो दगुर्छ—euta patho dagurchha
One lamb runs.

दुइटा पाठा दगुर्छन्—duita patha dagurchhan
Two lambs run,

तैं असल किताब किन्छस्— tan asal kitab kinchhas
Thou buyest a good book.

तिमी असल किताब किन्छौ—timi asal kitab kinchhau
You buy a good book.

एउटा फूल फुल्छ—euta phul phulchha
A flower blooms.

फूलहरू फुल्छन—phulharu phulchhan
Flowers bloom.

त्यो जान्छ—tyo janchha
He goes.

उनी जान्छन – uni janchhan
He goes (honorific sense)

गोपाल कृष्ण हरू पछाडि हटेनन्— Gopal krishan haru pa-
                                            chhadi hatenan
Gopal krishan and his men did not retreat.

Exercise

1. Write the plurals of :—

   छानु, नानी, मानिस, लडका, भ्यागुतो, पोको, तँ ।

2. Translate into Nepali :—

   Strong boys, Three sons. Ten rupees. One bow. Bad girls Ram and others. Hundred frogs. Beautiful child. Blind women.

LESSON—12

Case—कारक (karak)

A case is the relation of a noun or pronoun to the verb.

There are eight cases in Nepali, expressed by different post-positions or case endings. The post-positions mostly correspond to English prepositions. They come after a word and hence their name. The post-positions or the case-endings are as given below :

Name of the cas	Name of the post position	Sign.
1. कर्ताकारक (Nominative case)	प्रथमा	0, ले, बाट
2. कर्मकारक Objective case	द्वितीया	लाई
3. करणकारक (Instrumental case)	तृतीया	ले, बाट
4. सम्प्रदानकारक (Dative case)	चतुर्थी	लाई, के
5. अपादानकारक (Ablative case)	पञ्चमी	बाट, देखिन्
6. सम्बन्धकारक (Possessive case)	षष्ठो	को, का, की
7. अधिकरणकारक (Locative case)	सप्तमी	मा
8. सम्बोधनकारक (Vocative case)	—	हे, हो, ए, भो

85

1. The nominative case signifies the doer of some action ; as :—

लडका हाँस्छ —The boy laughs.

त्यो सुत्छ—He sleeps.

गाई सुस्ताउँछिन्—The cow rests.

In these sentences लडका, त्यो and गाई are nominatives to the verbs हाँस्छ, सुत्छ and सुस्ताउँछिन respectively. These nominatives have no case-ending with them.

There are two kinds of instances in which the nominative case-ending ले is omitted :—

(a) After the nominatives of all the intransitive verbs ; as::—

हामी जान्छौ – We go.

तिमी रोयौ—You wept.

प्रेम बस्ला—Prem will sit.

(b) After the nominatives of the transitive verbs in all tenses except the past tense ; as :—

लडकी पुस्तक पढछ —The girl reads a book·

त्यसेल काम गछ—He does his work.

बाखरी ले घाँस खान्छिन—The goat eats grass.

In this case, however, the case ending may optionally be used ; as :—

लडकीले पुस्तक पढछ—The girl reads a book.

त्यसले काम गर्छ – He does his work.

बाखरी ले घाँस खान्छिम—The goat eats grass.

Another nominative case ending वाट is used in the honorific sense ; as :—

राम हुकूम भयो—The Ram commanded.

बुबाबाट गनु हुनेछ—My father will do it,

2. The objective or accusative case (कर्मकारक) denotes the object of the transitive verb ; as :—

चिटठी लेख—Write a letter.

त्यो आँप खान्छ—He eats a mango.

Here चिटठी and आँप are in the objective case governed by the transitive verbs लेख and खान्छ respectively. These objectives have no case-endings with them.

There are two kinds of instances in which the objective case-ending लाई is omitted —

(a) After all the nouns denoting inanimate

objects as well as other than human beings ; **as—**

त्यो किताब फ्यांकिदेऊ—Throw away that book.

कालेले हिजो दुइटा खसी काटयो—Kale butchered two goats yesterday.

(b) After the direct objects ; as —

त्यसले मलाई दुह रुपैया दियो—He gave me two rupee.

गुरुले शिष्यलाई वेद पढायो—The teacher taught his disciple the Vedas.

Some special uses of the Second case-ending लाई

(a) In the sense of feeling or perception :—

तिमीलाई के मयो—What has happened to you ?

मेरो कुरा उसलाई राम्रो लागेन—My word did not satisfy him.

(b) In the sense of gain or loss :

पूजामा कृष्णलाई एउटा घड़ी फाइदा भयो—Krishan has got a watch in the Puja occasion.

रामलाई केही फाइदा भएन—Ram did not get anything.

3. The instrumental case (करणकारक) by which an action is done has the sign ले, बाट or द्वारा which means by, with, through, etc. ; as :—
कलमले लेख —Write with a pen.

यो काम तिमीबाटं हुँदैन—This work cannot be done by you

म यो शामद्वारा गराउँछु—I shall get it done through Shyam.

Some Special Uses of the Third Case-ending

(a) In the sense of cause :—

धनले धर्म हुँदैन—Virtue is not gained through wealth.

विद्याबाट विनय हुन्छ— Learning begets modesty.

(b) In the passive voice :—

मबाट अरु हिंडिदैन—I can't walk more.

यो काम उसबाट सम्पन्न भयो—This work was done by him.

(c) In the adverbial sense ;—

एक मीठोले बाहिर गयो—He went out on a sweet,

सस्तो भाउले किनें—I bought at cheap rate.

4. The dative case (सम्प्रदानकारक) denotes the person or thing for which the work is done, लाई (to), को लागि, को निमित्त (for) are the signs of the fourth case-ending.

बाहुनलाई भात देऊ—Give rice to the Brahmin·

घोडालाई चना ख्याऊ—Bring gram for the horse.

तपाई को लागि म अरू के गनं सक्छ ?—What more can I do for you ?

मेरो निम्ततपाई यति पनि गनं सक्नुहुन्न ?—Can you not do
even this for me.

Some Special Uses of the Fourth
Case-ending लाई and के

(a) In the sense of oblation :—

अग्नि-देवतालाई स्वाहा—These offerings are to the god
of Fire !

(b) In the sense of wishing well :—

तिमीलाई सुख होसू—May you be happy !

(c) In the sense of benediction, account of
expenditure, address etc. :—

छोरालाई आशीष—Blessings to the son !

गोपालके गएको सय रुपैया—Hundred rupees debited
to the account of Gopal.

अड्डाके पुर्जी—A letter to the office.

5. The ablative case (अपादानकारक) denotes
separation or reaction from something. The
post-positions देखि. देखिन, and बाट are its signs;
as :—

रूखबाट पात झछंन—Leaves fall from the tree.

त्यो आठ दिनदेखि चूप छ—He has been observing
silence since eight days.

मदेखि नरिसाऊ—Do not get angry with me.

त्यो बाघदेखिन डराउँछ—He fears from a tiger.

6. The possessive or genitive case (सम्बन्ध-कारक) shows the possessor of something. The post-positions को, का, की (of) are its signs. In the first and second persons रो, रा, रीं or नो, ना, नी are used in place of को, का, कीं respectively; as :—

रामको छोरो   (Ram's son) (masc. singular)

रामका छोराहरू   (Ram's sons) masc. plural)

रामकी छोरी   (Ram's daughter) (fem. singular)

रामका छोरीहरू   (Ram's daughters) (fem. plural)

मेरो एक भाइ   (A brother of mine) (masc. singular)

मेरा चार भाइ   (Four brothers of mine) (masc. plu.)

मेरी बहिनी   (My sister) fem. singular)

मेरा बहिनीहरू   (My sisters) (fem. plural)

आपनो छोरो   (own son) (masc. singular)

आपना छोराहरू   (own sons) masc. plural)

आपनी छोरी   (own daughter) (fem. singular)

आपना छोरीहरू   (own daughters) (fem, plural)

को is used before a singular masculine noun; का before a plural noun, whether masculine or feminine; and की is used before a singular feminine noun. Similar is the case with रो, रा, री and

नो, ना, नी. Hence the use of possessive post-positions depends on the noun possessed and not on the noun in the possessive case.

Possessive case is used as an adjective to the possessed noun. So it is formed according to the number and gender of the noun possessed,

7. The locative case (अधिकरणकारक) signifies the place, time or subject at which the action takes place. The post-position or case ending मा (in, on, upon, etc.) is used as its sign.

म यो घरमा रहन्छु—I live in this house.

तिम्रो हातमा के छ—What is in your hand ?

बाटोमा घेरै भीड छ—There is a large crowd on the road.

रूखमा नचढ—Don't climb up the tree.

पढनमा मन लगाऊ—Attend to your studies.

With the nouns signifying time and place, the case-ending मा may optionally by omitted; as :—

हामी घर (or घरमा) जान्छौं —We go home.

मेरो घर पूर्व (or पूर्वमा) छ—My house is to the east.

राम साँझ (or साँझमा) निरक्यो—Ram went out in the evening.

रूख (or रूखमा) नचढ—Don't climb up the tree.

Some Special Uses of the Seventh Case-ending

(a) In the sense of 'among', 'prompt', 'expert', 'addicted', 'clever', 'comparison' etc. :—

चरामा काग चख हुन्छ—The crow is the cleverest among the birds.

सिपाहीं काममा तत्पर हुन्छ—The soldier is prompt in action.

त्योबोलनमा सिपालु छ— He is expert in speaking.

राम जुवामा लग्नु छ—Ram is addicted to gambling.

(b) In the sense of contrast :—

कालो टोपीमा रातो फूल सुहाउँदैन—A red flower does not match a black cap.

8. The vocative case or the case of address (सम्बोधनकारक) denotes the persons addressed.

Its sign हो is generally omitted in the case of singular noun, whereas in the case of plural nouns it may optionally be used after them ; as :—

गोपाल, तिमी कहिले आयौं ?—Gopal when have you come ?

लडकाहरू (or लडकाहरू हो), तिमीहरू के गरिरहेका छौ ?—
Oh boys, what are you doing ?

परमेश्वर, दया गर—Oh God, be kind to us.

साथी श्रापनो सब हाल बताऊ—Oh friend, tell me all
your news.

In these sentences गोपाल, लडकाहरू, परमेश्वर and
साथी are in the vocative case.

PRONOUNS

Some pronouns change their forms when
added with the case-endings ; as :—

म—
   मैंले (I)

   मेरो, मेरा, मेरी (my)

ते—
   तैंले (thou)

   तेरो, तेरा, तेरी (thy)

तो—
   तिनले (she)

   तिनको, तिनका, तिनकी (her)
   तिनलाई (her)

उ—
   उनले (he or she)

   उनको, उनका, उनकी (his or her)
   उनलाई (him or her)

यी—
   यिनले (he or she)

   यिनको, यिनका, यिनकी (his or her)
   यिनलाई (him or her)

त्यसले (he)
त्यसलाई (him)

त्यो—

त्यसबाट (from him)
त्यसको (his) etc.

यसले (he)
यसलाई (him)

यो—

यसबाट (from him)
यसको (his) etc.

उसले (he)
उसलाई (him)

उ—

उसबाट (from him)
उसको (his) etc.

कसले (who)
कसलाई (whom)

को—

कसबाट (from whom)
कसको (whose) etc.

जसले (who)
जसलाई (whom)

जो—

जसबाट (from whom)
जसको (whose) etc.

Exercise

1. Correct the following by showing reasons :

यदुले गयो । लडकाले सुत्यो । सीता किताब ह्याइन । त्यो भोलि साँझमा आउला । सीताकी छोरा । गीताकी हातले । मेरा घरका छाना । तेरो बहिनीको छोरीं । कालेले खसीलाई काठ्यो । हिजो म भात खाएको देख्ता भाइले छक्क परयो ।

2. Fill up the gaps with case endings :—

म—रोटी खाँ । उ—काम गर्‍यो । तिमी—के भयो । लडका— लडकी—देख्यो । हरि घोडा—माया गर्दैन । यो किताब उ—देऊ । म— आरु हिंडिदन । त्यो बोल्न—सिपालु छ । गाई—घाँस ल्याऊ । लटठी— पिट । लोभ – पाप बढछ ।

3. Translate into Nepali :—

I have taken (खाए) rice. He has purchased (किनेको छ) a horse. What shall I bring (ल्याऊ) for you ? What are you doing (गरिरहेको) on the road ? Climb up the tree. Ram's mother. Rahim's sister. Sita's son. Gita's brother. Please wait a bit.

———

LESSON—13

DECLENSION OF NOUNS

नामहरूको रूपावली (Namharuko rupawali)

The mode of declension of a noun depends on its ending.

In Nepali all nouns end in vowels. A few examples of declension of nouns according to their different vowelendings are given here :

Declension of nouns ending in अ :—

बालक (Boy)

Masculine

Case	Singular	Plural
1. Nom.	बालक, बालकले a boy	बालक, बालकहरूले boys
2. Obj	बालक, बालकलाई a boy or to a boy	बालक, बालकहरूलाई boys or to boys
3. Inst.	बालकले by a boy	बालकहरूले by boys
4. Dative	बालकलाई, बालकके to a boy	बालकहरूलाई, -के to boys

बालकको लागि   बालकहरूको लागि
for a boy   for boys

5. Ablative बालकदेखि, -देखिन्, बालकहरूदेखि,
                      -बाट   -देखिन्,-बाट
        from a boy   from boys

6. Poss.   बालकको, -की, -का   बालकहरूको, -की, -का
        of a boy   of boys

7. Locative. बालकमा   बालकहरूमा
        in or on a boy   in or on boys

8. Voca.   हे बालक   हे ओ बालकहरू हो
        Oh boy   Oh boys

All nouns (irrespective of genders) ending in अ as बाघ (tiger), नन्द (sister-in-law), घर (house), etc. are declined like बालक।

The case-ending की is used when it is follo-wed by a feminine noun in the singular number;; का is used when followed by a plural noun ; as:—

हरिकी छोरी—Hari's daughter.

हरिका छोराहरू—Hari's sons.

Declension of Nouns Ending in आ

लडका (Boy)

Masculine

Case	Singular	Plural
1. Nom.	लडका, लडकाले a boy	लडकाहरू, लडकाहरूले boys
2. Obj.	लडका, लडकालाई a boy or to a boy	लडकाहरू, लडकाहरूलाई boys or to boys
3. Inst.	लडकाले by a boy	लडकाहरूले by boys
4. Dative	लडकालाई, के to a boy लडकाको लागि, निम्ति for a boy	लडकाहरूलाई -के to boys लडकाहरूको लागि, निम्ति for boys
5. Ablative	लडकादेखि, -देखिन, -बाट from a boy	लडकाहरूदेखि, देखिन -बाट from boys
6. Poss.	लडकाको, -का, -की, of a boy	लडकाहरूको, -का -की of boys
7. Locative	लडकामा in or on a boy	लडकाहरूमा in or on boys
8. Vocative	हे लडका oh boy	हे श्रो लडकाहरू हो oh boys

All nouns ending in आ irrespective of their genders as घोडा (horse), आमा (mother), पखा (fan) etc. are declined like लडका ।

Declension of Nouns Ending in इ

मुनि (Sage)

Masculine

Case	Singular	Plural
1. Nom.	मुनि, मुनिले a sage	मुनि, मुनिहरूले sages
2. Obj.	मुनि मुनिलाई a sage or to a sage	सुनि, मुनिहरूलाई sages or to sages
3. Inst.	मुनिले by a sage	मुनिहरूले by sages
4. Dative.	मुनिलाई, -के to a sage मुनिको लागि, -निम्ति for a sage	मुनिहरूलाई, -के to sages मुनिहरूको लागि, -निम्ति for sages
5. Ablative	मुनिदेखि, -देखिन्, -बाट from a sage	मुनिहरूदेखि, देखिन्, -बाट from sages
6. Poss.	मुनिको, -का, -की of a sage	मुनिहरूको, -की, -का of sages

7. Locative मुनिमा   मुनिहरूमा
       in or on a sage   in or on sages

8. Vocative हे मुनि   हे मुनिहरू हो
       Oh sage   Oh sages.

All nouns ending in इ or ई as भाइ (brother), छोरी (daughter), उर्दी (order) etc. are declined like मुनि ।

Only the long ई in the vocative case is changed into short इ if no addition is made to the noun ending in ई ; as :—

विद्यार्थी — student. विद्यार्थि — Oh student !

Declension of Nouns Ending in उ and ऊ

बाउ (father)

Masculine (ending in उ)

Case	Singular	Plural
1. Nom.	बाउ, बाउले a father	बाउ बाउहरूले fathers
2. Obj.	बाउ, बाउलाई to a father	बाउ बाउहरूलाई to fathers
3. Inst.	बाउले by a father	बाउहरूले by fathers

Case	Singular	Plural
4. Dative	बाउलाई, -के to a father बाउको लागि, –निम्ति for a father	बाउहरूलाई, -के to fathers बाउहरूको लागि, -निम्ति for fathers
5. Ablative	बाउदेखि -देखिन्, -वाट from a father	बाउहरूदेखि, देखिन्, -बाट from fathers
6. Poss,	बाउको, की, का of a father	बाउहरुको, की का of fathers
7. Locative	बाउमा in or on a father	बाउहरूमा in or on fathers
8. Voca.	हे बाउ Oh father	हे, श्रो वाहरूहो Oh fathers

All nouns ending in उ and ऊ as गोरू (ox), गाउँ (village), धनु (bow) and बुबाज्यू etc are declined like बाउ ; only the long ऊ in the Vocative Case is changed into short उ. But the gerundial nouns as well as the nouns of the neuter gender ending in नु are declined like छानु.

छानु (Roof)
Neuter

Case	Singular	Plural
1. Nom.	छानु, छानाले a roof	छाना, छानाहरूले roofs
2. Obj.	छानु, छानालाई to a roof	छानाहरू छानाहरूलाई to roofs
3. Inst.	छानाले by a roof	छानाहरूले by roofs
4. Dative	छानालाई, -के to a roof छानाको लागि, -निम्ति for a roof	छानाहरूलाई, -के to roofs छानाहरूको लागि, -निम्ति for roofs
5. Ablative	छानादेखि, -देखिन्, -बाट from a roof	छानाहरूदेखि, -देखिन्, -बाट from roofs
6. Poss.	छानाको, की, का of a roof	छानाहरूको, -की, -का of roofs
7. Locative	छानामा in or on a roof	छानाहरूमा in or on roofs

Case	Singular	Plural
8. Vocative	हे छानु !	हे, श्रो छानाहरू हो !
	Oh roof	Oh `roofs

All nouns ending in ए, ऐ, श्रो like बाज्ये (grand-father), बज्ये (grandmother), जौ (barley) etc. are declined like बालक ।

Declension of Nouns Ending in श्रो
छोरो (Son)
Masculine (पुलिग)

Case	Singular	Plural
1. Nam.	छोरो, छोरोले, छोरांले	छोरा, छोराहरूले
	a son	sons
2. Obj.	छोरो, छोरोलाई, छोरालाई	छोराहरू, छोराहरूलाई
	to a son	to sons
3. Inst.	छोरोले, छोराले	छोराहरूले
	by a son	by sons
4. Dative	छोरोलाई, के, छोरालाई, -के	छोराहरूलाई, के
	to a son	to sons
	छोरो, छोराको लागि, निम्ति	छोराहरूको लागि, निम्ति
	for a son	for sons

Case	Singular	Plural
5. Ablative	छोरो or छोरादेखि, -देखिन्, -बाट from a son	छोराहरूदेखि, देखिन्, -बाट from sons
6. Poss.	छोरो or छोराको, -की, -का of a son	छोराहरूको, -की, –का of sons
7. Locative	छोरोमा, छोरामा in or on a son	छोराहरूमा in or on sons
8. Vocative	हे छोरो Oh son	हे, श्रो छोराहरू हो Oh sons

All other noun ending in श्रो as केटो (boy), खोलो (stream), डांडो (hill) etc. are declined as छोरो ।

Nouns Ending in Consonants

Nouns ending in consonants as विद्वान (scholar), जगत (world) etc. are all from Sanskrit. They are declined like बालक ।

Examples

रमा बाउलाई बोलाउँछन्—Rama is calling his father.

त्यो बालकलाई नपिट—Don't beat that boy,

चम्चाले भात खाऊ—Eat rice with a spoon.

रमेश सियोले लुगा सिउँछिन—Ramesh sews cloth
with a needle.

बाखरी घाँस ल्याऊ—Bring grass for the goat.

अन्धालाई एक चिया देऊ—Give a tea to the blind
man.

गंगा हिमालयबाट निस्कन्छ—The Ganges comes out
of the Himalayas.

रमाको सानो भाइ आएको थियो—Rama's younger
brother had come.

सीताकी दिदी स्कूलकी शिक्षिका हुनू—Sita's elder sister
is a school teacher.

घरमा कोही छैन—There is none in the house.

पलंगमा लेटनुहोस—Please lie down on the bed-
stead.

लडकी हो ! अब तिमीहरू घर जान सक्छौ—Oh girls
you may go home now.

अरे दुष्ट ! तेरो दिन खतम मइरहे को छ—Oh villain
your days are coming to an end.

Exercise

1. Decline :—

नदी, मानिस, छानु, केटो, नन्द, भगवान and गुरु in the
2nd, 4th and 6th case-endings.

2. Correct the following ।—

छोरोहरूमा । हे विद्यार्थी । छानुदेखि, पाँच भाइ । रामको बहिनी । हरि भात खायो । हिजो कालेले दुइटा खसीलाई काट्यो । डाँडोहरूवाट नदी भच्छ ।

3. Translate into Nepali :—

Boys are playing. Two girls have come from Punjab. The king lives in a palace. Cows eat leaves and branches of trees. Men are slaves of habit. The fruit fell from the tree. Give land to the landless. The water of the sea is saline. Oh boys Don't go there.

———.

LESSON—14

DECLENSION OF PRONOUNS
सर्वनामको रूपावली (Sarvanamko Rupavali)
म—(I)
1st Person

Case	Singular	Plural
1. Nom.	म, मैंले I	हामीहरू, हामीहरूले, हामीहरूबाट we
2. Obj.	मलाई me	हामीहरूलाई us
3. Inst.	मैंले by me	हामींहरूले, हासीहरूबाट by us
4. Dative	मलाई to me	हामौहरूलाई, -के to us
5. Ablative	मदेखि, देखिन्, -वाट from me	हामीहरूदेखि, देखिन्, -बाट from us
6. Poss.	मेरो, मेरा, मेरी my, mine	हाम्रो, हाम्रा, हाम्री, हामीहरूको, -का, -की our, ours

108

Case	Singular	Plural
7. Locative	ममा in or on me	हामीहरूमा in or on us

N. B. Pronouns have no vocative case.

तैं —(Thou)
2nd Person

Case	Singular	Plural
1. Nom.	तैं, तैंले thou	तिमीहरू तिमीहरूले you
2. Obj.	तैंलाई three	तिमीहरूलाई you
3, Inst,	तैंले by thee	तिमीहरूले by you
4, Dative	तैंलाई to thee	तिमीहरूलाई, -के to you
5, Ablative	तंदेखि, देखिन, -बाट from thee	तिमीहरूदेखि, देखिन -बाट from you
6. Poss.	तेरो, तेरा, तेरी तिम्रो तिम्रा तिम्री thy, thine	तिमीहरूको, तिमीहरूका, तिमीहरूकी your, yours

Case	Singular	Plural
7. Locative	तँमा	तिमीहरुमा
	in or on thee	in or on you

N.B. Of all pronouns in the possessive case those ending in को, का, की, or रो, रा, री are used when followed by singular, plural and singular feminine nouns respectively.

तपाई — (You)

Second Person (respectful)

Case	Singular	Plural
1. Nom.	तपाई, तपाई ले, -बाट	तपाई हरु, पातई हरुले, -बाट
2. Obj.	तपाई लाई	तपाईहरुलाई
3. Inst.	तपाई ले -बाट	तपाई हरुले —बाट
4. Dative	तपाई लाई -के	तपाई हरुलाई -के
5. Ablative	तपाई देखि, देखिन, -बाट	तपाईहरुदेखि, देखिन, -बाट
6. Poss.	तपाई को -की, -का	तपाई हरुको, -की, -का
7. Locative	तपाई मा	तपाई हरुमा

त्यो—(He, she)
Third Person

Case	Singular	Plural
1. Nom.	त्यो, सो, त्यसले त्यल्ले he, she	तो, तिनीहरु, तिनीहरूले they
2. Obj.	त्यो, सो, त्यसलाई, त्यल्लाई him, her	ती, तिनीहरू, तिनीहरूलाई them
3. Inst.	त्यसले, त्यल्ले by him or her	तिनीहरूले by them
4. Dative	त्यसलाई, -के, त्यल्लाई to or for him, her	तिनीहरूलाई, -के to or for them
5 Ablative	त्यसदेखि, देखिन, -बाट from him or her	तिनीहरूदेखि, देखिन, -बाट from them
6. Poss.	त्यसको, -की, -का his or her	तिनीहरूको, -की, -का their
7. Locative	त्यसमा in or on him, her	तिनीहरूमा in or on them

N.B. When used in the honorific sense त्यो is changed into तिनी and declined as follows ।—

तिनी He (respectful)

Third person

Case	Singular	Plural
1. Nom.	तिनीं तिनीलें तिनलें he or she	तो तिनीहरू तिनीहरूलें they
2. Obj.	तिनीलाई, तिनलाई him or her	ती, तिनीहरू, तिनीहरूलाई them
3. Inst.	तिनीले, निनले by him or her	तिनीहरूले by them
4. Dative	तिनीलाई, -के तिनलाई, -के to or for him, her	तिनीहरूलाई, -के to them
5. Ablative	तिनी or तिनदेखि, देखिन, -बाट from him or her	तिनीहरूदेखि, -देखिन -वांट from them
6. Poss.	तिनी or तिनको, -की, -का his or her	तिनीहरूको, -की, -का their

Case	Singular	Plural
7. Locative	तिनी or तिनमा in or on him, her	तिनीहरूमा in or on them

यो—This, It
Third Person

Case	Singular	Plural
1. Nom.	यो, यसले यल्ले this or it	यी, यिनीहरू, यिनीहर न these
2. Obj.	यो, यसलाई यल्लाई this or it	यो, यिनीहरू यिनीहरूलाई these
3. Inst.	यसले, यल्ले by this or it	निनीहरूले by these
4. Dative	यसलाई,-के,यल्लाई to or for this	यिनीहरूलाई, -के to or for them
5. Ablative	यसदेखि, देखिन, -बाट from this	यिनीहरूदेखि, देखिन, -बाड from them
6. Poss.	यसको, -की,-का of this or it	यिनीहरूकी, -की, -का of these

Case	Singular	Plural
7. Locative	यसमा in or on this, it	यिनीहरूमा in or on these

N.B. When used in the honorific sense यो is changed into यिनी and declined as तिनी

उ—He
Third Person

Case	Singular	Plural
1. Nom.	उ, उसले, उल्ले he	ऊ, उनीहरू, उनीहरूल they
2. Obj.	उ, उसलाई, उल्लाई him	ऊ, उनीहरू, उनीहरूलाई them
3. Inst.	उसले, उल्ले by him	उनोहरूले by them
4. Dative	उसलाई, -के, उल्लाई to or for him	उनीहरूलाई. -के to or for them
5. Ablative	उसदेखि, देखिन, -बाट from him	उनीहरूदेखि, देखिन, -बाट from them
6. Poss.	उसको, -की, -का his	उनीहरूको, -की, -का their

Case	Singular	Plural
7. Locative	उसमा	उनीहरूमा
	in or on him	in or on them

N.B. When used in the honorific sense, उ is changed into उनी and declined like तिनी

आफू—Self

Case	Singular	Plural
1. Nom.	आफू, आफूले, -बाट self	आफूहरू, आफूहरूल, -बाट selves
2. Obj.	आफूलाई to self	आफूहरूलाई to selves
3. Inst.	आफूले, -बाट by self	आफूहरूले, -बाट by selves
4. Dative	आफूलाई to or for self	आफूहरूलाई to or for selves
5. Ablative	आफूदेखि, देखिन, -बाट from self	आफूहरूदेखि, देखिन, -बाट from selves
6. Poss.	आफनो, आफनी, आफना of self	आफनो, आफनी, आफना, आफूहरूको, -की -का, of selves

Case	Singular	Plural
7. Locative	म्राफूमा	म्राफूहरूमा
	in self	among selves

कोही—One any one
Always Singular

1. Nom.   कोहीं, कसैले (one or any one)
2. Obj.   कोही, कसैलाई (to one or any one)
3. Inst.   कसैले (by one or any one)
4. Dative   कसैलाई (to or for any one)
5. Ablative कसैबाट (from one or any one)
6. Poss.   कसको, –की, -का (of one or any one)
7. Locative कसैमा (in, on one or any one)

के—What (interrogative)

(Always neuter and singular)

1. Nom.   के, केले   2. Obj.   के, केलाई
3. Inst.   केले   4. Dative केलाई
5. Ablative केदेखि, देखिन, बाट 6. Poss. केको, –की, –का
7. Locative केमा

जो—Who, which (Relative)

Case	Singular	Plural
1. Nom,	जो, जुन, जसले, -बाट, जल्ले	जो, जुन, जुनले
	who, which	who, which

Case	Singular	Plural
2. Obj.	जो, जुन, जसलाई, जस्लाई whom, which	जो, जुन, जुनले whom, which
3. Inst.	जसले, बाट, जल्ले by whom or which	जुनले, -बाट by whom or which
4. Dative	जसलाई, के, जल्लाई to or for whom	जुनलाई के to or for whom
5. Ablative	जसदेखि, देखिन, -बाट from whom	जुनदेखि, देखिन, -बाट from whom
6. Poss.	जसको, की, का of which, whose	जुनको, की, का of which, whose
7. Locative	जसमा in or on whom	जुनमा in or on whom

जे—What (Relative)
(Always neuter, singular)

1. Nom.	जे, जेले	2. Obj.	जे, जेलाई
3. Inst.	जेले	4. Dative	जेलाई
5. Ablative	जेदेखि, देकिन, बाट		
6. Poss.	जेको, की, का	7. Locative	जेमा

को—Who, which, (Interrogative)

Case	Singular	Plural
1. Nom.	कौ, कुन, कसले, कल्ले who, which	को कुन कुनले who, which
2. Obj.	को, कुन, कसलाई, कल्लाई whom, which	को कुन, कुनलाई whom, which
3. Inst.	कसले, बाट, कल्ले by whom	कुनले, बाट by whom
4. Dative	कसलाई, के, कल्लाई to or for whom	कुनलाई, के to or for whom
5. Ablative	कसदेखि, देखिन, -बाट from whom	कुनदेखि, देखिन, -ब:ट from whom
6. Poss.	कसको, -की, -का whose, of which	कुनको, -की, -का whose, of which
7. Locative	कसमा in or on whom	कुनमा in or on whom

Uses of तं, तिमी and तपाई

तं (thou) is used in speaking to God and persons inferior to the speaker; as :—

हे ईश्वर म तेरो शरणमा छु—O God ! I am in Thy care.

तँ फाटाहा होस, तलाई कसरी विश्वास गरूँ—You are a liar
how can I believe you?

तिमीं (you) denotes familiarity, and is used
between equals; as :—

तिमी के चाहन्छौ—What do you want ?

तिमीबाट के लुकाऊ—What should I hide from you?

तपाई (you) is used in showing respect or cour-
tesy ; as :—

कृपागरी तपाई यहाँ ग्राउनुहोस—Please come here.

तपाईं एकै छिन बस्नुहोस—Please sit down for a
while.

ग्राफू (self) is used as a reflexive pronoun in
nominative case without ले ; as :—

तिमी ग्राफैं त्यहाँ जान सक्छौ—You yourself can go
there.

स्वयं (self) is often used instead of the reflexive
pronoun ग्राफू ; as :—

उ स्वयं यहाँ ग्रायो—He himself has come here.

The forms ग्राफ्नो and ग्राफ्नै are used as pronouns in the possessive case to mean one's own ;
as :—

त्यो मेरो ग्राफ्नो घर हो—This is my own house.

त्यो ग्राफ्नै किताब पढछ—He reads his own book.

आफू आपना or आपना.आपना is used in the sense of respective ; as :—

लड़काहरु आपना आपना घर गए—The boys went to their respective houses.

The form आफस is used in the possessive and locative plurals only ; as :—

तिमीहरुको आपसको प्रेम देखर त्यो बिलकुलै सुग्ध भयौ—He was totally charmed to see your love (the love among yourselves).

तिमीहरु आपसमा किन बाभिरहेछौ ?—Why are you quarrelling among yourselves ?

Uses of को and के

को is used for persons and के for inanimate objects ; as :—

को आउ दे छ ?—Who comes there ?

तिमी के खान चाह्न्छौ ?—What do you want to eat?

के is used adverbially to introduce an interrogative sentence ; as :—

के तपाई यहाँ बस्नुहुन्छ —Will you stay here ?

के is also used in the sense of astonishment ; as :—

के हो यसिको हल्ला किन —What is the matter! Why there is so much noise ?

के is sometimes used as whether or ; as :—

के घर के बाहिर—Whether in the house or out-side it.

The uses of कोही and केही

कोही means some one or any one, and केही means something or a few. Generally कोही refers to a person and केही to a thing ; as —

कोही आएनं - No one came.

कोही न कोही त्यहां गयो—Some one or other went there.

केही त खाऊ—Take a little at least.

केही दिन अगाडि तिम्रो कपडा पाए—Received your cloth a few days ago.

कोही-कोही means a few, some etc. ; as :—

कोही-कोही यस्तो मन्छन—Some people say like this.

कोही is used idiomatically as an adverb and means about or nearly ; as :—

कोही पन्ध्रबीस मानिस यहां आए—About fifteen or twenty persons came here.

Examples ;—

तिम्रो नाम के हो ?—What is your name ?

मेरो नाम राम हो — My Name is Ram

उसको नाम के हो — What is his name ?

उसको नाम रमेश हो — His name is Ramesh.

त्यहाँ को गएको थियो — Who had gone there ?

त्यहाँ कोही पनि गएको थिएन — No one had gone
there.

यो घरमा को बस्छ — Who lives in this house ?

यो घरमा मेरो भाइको साथी बस्छ — My brother's friend
lives in this house.

ग्राफ्नो काम ग्राफै गर — Do your work yourself.

मैले यो काम ग्राफैले गरें — I have done this work
myself.

उनी स्वयं यो काम गर्न सवछन् — He can do this work
himself.

म ग्राफ्नो ग्राँखाले यो हेर्न चाह्‌छु — I wish to see this
with my own eyes.

तिमको लागि केही त गर — Do something at least
for her.

Exercise

1. Decline : —

म, तैं, त्यो and यो in the 1st, 2nd, 4th and 6th
case-endings in singular and plural numbers;

को, जो and कोही in the 2nd, 6th and 7th case endings in both numbers.

2. Correct the following :—

हामींको भाइ । तिमीको छोरो । यसको छोरी । तिम्रो बहिनी । तेरो ग्रामा । हामीलाई कोले बोलायो । कसको भाइ ग्राएको थियो । सीताको छोरा जान्छ । गीताको ह्रातले । रमेशका छा्रोमा ।

3. Translate into Nepali :—

My son Your daughter. Her sister. In me. In them. To them. To whom. By us. By you. A few men. Whose house. This is my own house. They went to their respective houses Some one or other.

————

LESSON—15
CONJUGATION OF VERBS

क्रियापदको रूपावली (Kriyapadko rupavali)

There are three kinds of tenses in grammer :

(1)   Present tense,

(2)   Past tense, and

(3)   Future tense.

These three tenses are again divided into many divisions according to the rules of their conjugation.

हुनु (to be)

Present Tense

Person	Singular		Plural	
Ist.	मछु महँ	I am	हामी छौं हामी हौं	We are
2nd.	तैं छस तैं होस	Thou art.	तिमीहरू छौ तिमीहरू हौ	You are.

124

	त्यो छ	तिनीहरू छन
	त्यो हो	
3rd.	He is.	They are.
	उ छ	तिनीहरू हुन
	उ हों	

	तिनी छिन	तिनीहरूछन
	तिनी हुन	
3rd.	She is	They are
	उनी छिन	तिनीहरू हुन्
	उनी हुन	

Past Tense

Person	Singular	Plural
1st.	म थिए —I was.	हामीहरू थियौ We were.
2nd.	तं थिइस—Thou wast.	तिमीहरू थियौ—You were.

	त्यो थियो	
	तिनी थिए	
3rd.	He was.	तिनीहरू थिए— They were
	उ थियो	
	उनी थिए	

	त्यो थिई	
	निनी थिइन	
3rd.	She was	तिनीहरू थिए They were
	उ थिई	
	उनी थिइन	

Future Tense

Person	Singular	Plural
1st.	म हुनेछु—I shall be.	हामीहरू हुनेछौं—We shall be.
2nd.	तँ हुनेछस—Thou wilt be.	तिमीहरू हुनेछौ—You will be
3rd.	त्यो हुनेछ उ हुनेछ तिनीहुनेछन उनी हुनेछन — He will be.	तिनीहरू हुनेछन—They will be.

In Nepali there are three kinds of present tense ; (i) Present Indefinite (सामान्य वर्तमान्), (ii) Present Continuous (अपूर्ण वर्तमान) and (iii) Present Perfect (पूर्ण वर्तमान).

(i) A verb is said to be in the Present Indefinite Tense when it refers simply to an action of the present time ; as :—

म जान्छु—I go.   त्यो गर्छ—He does.

In these sentences जान्छु and गर्छ are verbs in the Present Indefinite Tense.

(ii) Present Continuous tense denotes that

the action of the verb is in progress at the present time, as :—

> म गइरहेको छु—I am going.

> त्यो आइरहेको छ—He is coming.

In these sentences गइरहेको छु and आइरहेको छ are verbs in the Present Continuous or Present Imperfect Tense.

(iii) Present Perfect Tense denotes that the action of the verb is in the completed or perfect state ; as :—

> म गएको छु—I have gone.

> त्यो आएको छ—He has come.

In these sentences गएको छु and आएको छ are verb in the Present Perfect Tense.

Past Tense

In Nepali there are four kinds of Past Tense as :—

(i) Past Indefinite (सामान्य भूत) ; (ii) Past Continuous (अपूर्ण भूत) ; (iii) Past Perfect (पूर्ण भूत) and (iv) Unknown Past (अज्ञात भूत).

(i) Past Indefinite Tense is formed by adding ए (1st person singular), यौं (1st person plural), इस (2nd person singular), यौ (2nd person plural), यौं (3rd person singular. masculine), ई (3rd person singular, feminine), इन (third person singular, feminine in the honorific sense) and ए (third person plural) to the root ; as :—

हाँस्नु (to laugh) Intransitive

1st Person

Singular	Plural
म हाँसे—I laughed.	हामीहरू हाँस्यौं—We laughed.

2nd Person

तैं हाँसिस—Thou didst laugh	तिमीहरू हाँस्यो—You
तिमी हाँस्यो—You laughed	laughed.

3rd Person

त्यो हाँस्यो—You laughed.	
तिनी हाँसिन—She laughed.	तिनीहरू हाँसे—They
त्यो हाँसी—She laughed.	laughed.

(ii) Past Continuous Tense is formed by adding इरहेको and then the past form of हुनु to the root ; as :—

Singular	Plural

1st Person

म हाँसिरहेको (की) थिए— I was laughing.	हामी हाँसिरहेका थियौं— We were laughing

Singular   Plural

2nd Person

तें हाँसिरहेको की थिइस—Thou
            wast laughing.   तिमीहरू हाँसिरहेका थियौं—
तिमी हाँसिरहेको (की) थियौ—   You were laughing.
    You were laughing.

3rd Person

त्यो हांसिरहेको थियो - He was
                laughing.
तिनी हाँसिरहेकी थिइन्—She was   तिनी हांसिरहेका थिए—
                laughing.   They were laughing
त्यो हांसिरहेकी थिई—She was
            laughing

(iii) Past Perfect Tense is formed by adding 'एको'
and then the past form of हुनु to the root ; as : —

1st Person

म हाँसेको (की) थिए —I had   हामी हाँसेका थियौं—We had
            laughed.   laughed.

2nd Person

त हाँसेको (की) थिइस—Thou
            hadst laughed.   तिमीहरू हांसेका थियो—You
तिमी हांसेको (की) थियौ—You   had laughed.
    had laughed.

Singular   Plural

3rd Person

त्यो हाँसेको थियो—He had
                laughed.

तिनी हाँसेकी थिइन—She had   तिनीहरू हाँसेका थिए—They
                laughed.   had laughed.

त्यां हाँसेकी थिई —She had
                laughed.

(iv) Unknown Past Tense is formed by adding 'ए' and 'इ' and then the present form of 'हुनु' to the root ; as :—

1st Person

Singular   Fem Sing.   Plural

म हाँसेछु   हाँसिछु   हामी हाँसेछौं
I happened to laugh.   We happened to laugh.

2nd Person

तं हाँसिछस   ×   तिमीहरू हाँसेछौं
Thou didst, happen to   You happened
laugh.   to laugh.

3rd Person

त्यो हाँसेछ   हाँसिछ   तिनीहरू हाँसेछन
He happened to laugh   They happened to
                             laugh

Future Tense

In Nepali Future Tense is also of four kinds : —

(i) (सामान्य भविष्यत काल Future Indefinite).

(ii) (अपूर्ण भविष्यत काल Future Continuous).

(iii) (पूर्ण भविष्यत काल Future Perfect).

(iv) (सम्भावना भविष्यत काल Future Conditional).

(i) (Future Indefinite Tense is formed by adding 'ने' and then the present form of हुनु to the root : as :—

1st Person

Singular   Plural

म हाँस्नेछु I shall laugh.   हामी हाँस्नेछौं We shall laugh.

2nd Person

तं हाँस्नेछस   तिमीहरू हाँस्नेछौ
Thou will laugh.   You will laugh.

3rd Person

त्यो हाँस्नेछ   तिनीहरू हाँस्नेछन
He will laugh,   They will laugh.

N. B. While emphasis in action, 'न्यं' is added instead of 'ने', as ;—म हांस्न्यैछु, त्यो जान्यैछ etc.

(ii) Future Continuous Tense is formed by adding 'इरहने' and then the present form of 'हुनु' to the root ; as ;—

1st Person

Singular	Plural
म हांसिरहनेछु	हामीहरू हांसिरहनेछौं
I shall be laughing	We shall be laughing

2nd Person

तं हांसिरहनेछस	तिमीहरू हांसिरहनेछौ
Thou wilt be laughing.	You will be laughing.

3rd Person

त्यो हांसिरहनेछ	तिनीहरू हांसिरहनेछन
He will be laughing.	They will be laughing.

(iii) Future Perfect Tense is formed by adding 'एको' and then the future form of 'हुनु' to the root ; as :—

1st Person

Singular	Plural
म हांसेको हुनेछु	हामी हांसेका हुनेछौं
I shall have laughed.	We shall have laughed.

2nd Person

तं हांसिको (की) हुनेछस
Thou wilt have laughed.

तिमीहरू हांसेका हुनेछौ
You will have laughed.

3rd Person

त्यो हांसिको (की) हुनेछ
He or she will have laughed.

तिनीहरू हांसेका हुनेछन
They will have laughed.

(iv) Future Conditional Tense (सम्भावना भविष्यत काल) is formed by उला, औला, उला etc. ; as :—

1st Person

Singular	Plural
म हांसुँला	हामी हांसौंला
I shall laugh.	We shall laugh.

2nd Person

तं हांस्ला (स्लि) स
Thou wilt laugh.

तिमीहरू हांसौला
You will laugh

3rd Person

त्यो हांस्ला
He will laugh.
तिनी हांस्लिन — She will laugh.

तिनीहरू हांस्लान
They will laugh.

Negative : अकरण (akaran)

Negative is formed by adding 'न' to the verb.

(i)   In the beginning ; as :—
नहांस—Do not laugh.

(ii) In the end ; as :—
त्यो हाँसेन— He did not laugh

(iii) तिमी हाँस्तैनथ्यो — You would not have
laughed.

Examples

कृष्ण, हिजो तिमी कहाँ गइरहेको थियौ—Krishan, where were
you going yesterday ?

म बजार गइरहेको थिए—I was going to the market.

तिमीसग अरु को-को गइरहेका थिए ?—Who else were going
with you ?

मसंग अरु दुइटा लडकी थिए—Two more Girls were with
me.

तिमीहरूले बजारबाट के-के किनेर ल्यायौ ?—What things did
you purchase from the market ?

हामीले बजारबाट चामल, दाल, साग, आदि किनेर ल्यायौं We
bought rice, pulse, vegetables etc. from the
market.

मलाई किन भनेनौ, म पनि तिमीसगै जान्थ्यें ?--**Why did you not inform me, I would have gone with you ?**

ग्रहो रमेश, कहिले ग्रायो ?—**Hallo Ramesh, when did you come ?**

मखैरै ग्राए ँ— **I have come just now.**

के तिम्रो साथी पजाब बाट फक्यां ँ ?—**Have your friend returned from Punjab ?**

ग्रायो होला, तर मैंले ग्रहिलेसम्म खबर पाएको छैन—**He might have come, but I am not yet informed.**

के त्यो दिन तिमीले देवकोटाजीलाई भेटन पायौ—**Could you manage to see Devkotaji that day ?**

के मनेको, देवकोटाजी त त्योदिन हाम्रा घरमा ग्राउनु भएको थियो—**What do you say, that day Devkotaji had come to our house.**

के उहाँसंग तिम्रो केही कुरा भयो - **Have you had any talk with him ?**

जरूर, मैंले उहाँसँग ग्राठ मिनेट कुरा गर्न पाएको थिए ँ - **Oh yes I could have a talk with him for Eight minutes.**

Exercise

1. Conjugate : —

Verb हुनु (to be) in the Present, Future and Past Tense in both numbers ; verb जानु (to go) and verb हाँस्नु (to laugh) in the Present Indefinite

Tense (सामान्य वर्तमान), Future Indefinite Tense
(सामान्य भविष्यत काल), Past Indefinite (सामान्य भूत)
ane Future Conditional Tense (सम्भावना भविष्यत) in
both numbers and genders.

2. Translate into Nepali :—

They go to school. You sit in the house.
He writes a latter. Sita sings a song Ram sews
a cloth. Where will you go ? They will come to
the village. Will he not do this work ? We were
walking. They were hearing his words (कुरा). You
had come in time. I have gone with you He will
have come. They had not gone. Why have you
not told me this ? I will be going.

————

CONJUGATION OF VERBS

क्रियापदको रूपावली

In Nepali Verbs are Transformed according to the number, gender and persons of their nominatives ; as ;—

1s Person	म दगुछुँ	I run.
	हामी दगुछौ	We run.
2nd Person	नैं दगुछंस	Thou runest.
	तिमीहरू दगुछौ	You run.
3rd Person	त्यो दगुछुँ	He runs.
	तिनी दगुछिन	She runs.
	तिनीहरू दगुछंन	They run.
Masculine	शाम दगुछुँ	Shyam runs.
Feminine	गीता दगुछिन	Gita runs.
Singular	घोडा दगुछुँ	A horse runs.
Plural	घोडाहरू दगुछंन	Horses run.

Verbs of the masculine nominatives in the first person, singular number differ in their forms

137

with those of the feminine nominatives in the same number and person in the Present Continuous, Present Perfect, Past Continuous, Past Perfect, Unknown Past and Future tense, whereas in the plural number and in other tenses they behave alike : as ;—

(i) **Present Continuous Tense—** (अपूरण वर्तमान काल)

(Masculine Subject—कर्त्ता पुलिंग)

Singular	Plural
I am laughing.	We are laughing.
म हांसिरहेको छु	हामी हांसिरहेका छौं

(Feminine Subject— कर्ता स्त्रीलिंग)

I am laughing.	We are laughing.
म हांसिरहेको छु	हांमी हासिरहेका छौं

(ii) **Present Perfect Tense** (पूरण वर्तमान काल)

(Masculine Subject—कर्त्ता पुलिंग)

I have laughed.	We have laughed.
म हांसेको छु	हामी हांसेका छो

(Feminine Subject—कर्ता स्त्रीलिंग)

I have laughed.	We have laughed.
म हांसेकी छु	हामी हांसेका छौ

(iii) Present Continuous Tense (अपूर्ण भूत काल)

(Masculine Subject—कर्ता पुलिंग)

I was laughing.
म हांसिरहेको थिए

We were laughing.
हामी हांसिरहेका थियौं

(Feminine Subject—कर्ता स्त्रीलिंग)

I was laughing.
म हांसिरहेकी थिए

We were laughing.
हामी हांसिरहेका थियौं

(iv) Past Perfect Tense (पूर्ण भूत काल)

(Masculine Subject—कर्ता पुलिंग)

I had laughed.
म हांसेको थिए

We had laughed.
हामी हांसेका थियौं

(Feminine Subject—कर्ता स्त्रीलिंग)

I had laughed.
म हांसेकी थिए

We had laughed.
हामी हांसेका थियौं

(v) Uuknown Past Tense (अज्ञात भूत काल)

(Masculine Subject—कर्ता पुलिंग)

I happened to laugh.
म हांसे छु

We happened to laugh.
हामी हांसेछौं

(Feminine Subject—कर्ता स्त्रीलिंग)

I happened to laugh.
म हांसिछु

We happened to laugh.
हामी हांसेछौं

(vi) Future Perfect Tense (पूर्ण भविष्यत काल)

(Masculine Subject—कर्ता पुलिग)

I shall have laughed.   We shall have laughed.
म हांसिको हुनेछु   हामी हांसेका हुनेछौ

(Feminine Subject— कर्ता स्त्रीलिग)

I shall have laughed.   We shall have laughed
म हांसेकी हुनेछु   हामी हांसेका हुनेछौं

(vii) Present Indefinite Tense (सामान्य वर्तमान काल)

(Masculine Subject—कर्ता पुलिग)

I laugh.   We laugh.
म हांस्छु   हामी हांस्छौं

(Feminine Subject—कर्ता स्त्रीलिग)

I laugh.   We laugh.
म हांस्छु   हामी हांस्छौ

(viii) Past Indefinite Tense (सामान्य भूत काल)

(Masculine Subject— कर्ता पुलिग)

I laughed.   We laughed.
म हांसें   हामी हांस्यौं

(Feminine Subject—कर्ता स्त्रीलिग)

I laughed.   We laughed.
म हांसें   हामी हांस्यौं

(ix) Future Indefinite Tense (सामान्य भविष्यत काल)

(Masculine Subject—कर्ता पु‌लिग)

I shall laugh.   We shall laugh.
म हांस्नेछु   हामी हांस्नेछौ

(Feminine Subject—कर्ता स्त्रीलिग)

I shall laugh.   We shall laugh.
म हांस्नेछु   हामी हांस्नेछौ

(x) Future Conditional Tense (संभावना भविष्यत काल)

(Masculine Subject— कर्ता पुलिग)

I shall laugh.   We shall laugh.
म हांसुं‌ला   हामी हाँपौला

(Feminine Subject—कर्ता स्त्रीलिग)

I shall laugh.   We shall laugh.
म हांसुला   हामी हांसौला

Verbs of the masculine nominatives in the second
and third persons, singular number differ in their forms
with those of the feminine nominatives in the same
number and persons in all the tenses except in the Future
Indefinite tense as well as the past Indefinite tense where
the verbs in the second person, singular number behave

alike in both the genders ; as :—

(i) Present Indefinite Tense

(सामान्य वर्तमान काल)

(Masculine Subject – कर्ता पुलिंग)

Second Person

Singular	Plural
Thou laughest.	You laugh.
त हाँस्छस	तिमीहरू हाँस्छौ
You laugh.	
तिमी हाँस्छौ	

Third Person

He laughs.	They laugh.
त्यो हांस्छ	तिनीहरू हांस्छन्
He laughs.	
तिनी हाँस्छन्	

(Feminine Subject—कर्ता स्त्रीलिंग)

Second Person

Singular	Plural
Thou laughest.	You laugh.
तं हांस्छेस	तिमीहरू हाँस्छौ
You laugh.	
तिमी हांस्छयौ	

Third Person

She laughs

त्यो हाँस्छे

She laughs.

तिनी हाँस्छिन

They laugh.

तिनीहरू हाँस्छन्

(ii) Present Continuous Tense

(अपूर्ण वर्तमान काल)

(Masculine Subject—कर्ता पूर्लिंग)

Second Person

Thou art laughing

तैं हाँसिरहेको छस

You are laughing.

तिमी हाँसिरहेका छौ

You are laughing.

तिमीहरू हाँसिरहेका छौ

Third Person

He is laughing.

त्यो हाँसिरहेको छ

He is laughing.

तिनी हाँसिरहेका छन्

तिनी हाँसिरहेका छन्

They are laughing.

(Feminine Subject— कर्ता स्रं लिग)

Second Person

Thou art laughing.
तं हांसिरहेकी छस

You are laughing.
तिमीहरू हांसिरहेका छौ

You are laughing.
तिमी हांसिरहैंकी छौ

3rd Person

She is laughing.
त्यो हांसिरहेकी छ

They are laughing.
तिनीहरू हांसिरहेका छन्

She is laughing.
तिनी हांसिरहेकी छन्

(iii) Present Perfect Tense (पूर्ण वर्तमानकाल)

(Masculine Subject—कर्त्ता पु लिग)

2nd Person

Singular   Plural

Thou hast laughed.   You have laughed.
तें हांसेको छस   तिमीहरू हांसेका छौ

You have laughed.
तिमी हांसेका छौ

Third Person

He has laughed.   They have laughed.
त्यो हांसेको छ   तिमीहरू हांसेका छन्

He has laughed.
तिनी हांसेका छन्

(Feminine Subject—कर्त्ता स्त्रीलिंग)

2nd Person

Thou **hast** laughed.
तं हांसेकी छस

You **have** laughed.
तिमीहरू हांसेका छौ

You **have** laughed.
तिमी हांसेकी छौ

3rd Person

She has laughed.
त्यो हांसेकी छ

They **have laughed.**
तिनीहरू हांसेका छन

She has laughed.
तिनीहासेकी छन

(iv) **Past Indefinite Tense** (सामान्य भूतकाल)

(Masculine Subject—कर्त्ता पुर्लिंग)

Second Person

Thou didst laugh.
तैं हाँसिस

You laughed.
तिमीहरू हांस्यौ

You laughed.
तिमी हांस्यौ

Third Person

He laughed.
त्यो हांस्यौ

They **laughed.**
तिनीहरू हाँसे

He laughed.
तिनी हांसे

(Feminine Subject—कर्त्ता स्त्रीलिंग)

Second Person

Singular

Thou didst laugh.
तैं हाँसिस

You laughed.
तिमी हांस्यौ

Plural

You laaghed.
तिमीहरू हास्यौ

Third Person

She laughed
त्यो हांसी

She laughed.
तिनी हासिन्

They laughed.
तिनीहरू हांसे

(v) Past Continuous Tense (अपूर्ण भूत काल)

(Masculine Subject—कर्त्ता पुंलिग)

Second Person

Singular

Thou wert laughing.
तैं हांसिरहेको थिइस

You were laughing.
तिमी हांसिरहेका थियौ

Plural

You were laughing.
तिमीहरू हांसिरहेका थियौ

Third Person

He was laughing.　They were laughing.
त्यो हाँसिरहेको थियो　तिनीहरू हाँसिरहेका थिए

He was laughing.
तिनी हाँसिरहेका थिए

(Feminine Subject—कर्ता स्त्रीलिंग)
2nd Person

Thou wert laughing　You were laughing.
तैं हाँसिरहेकी थिइस्　तिमीहरू हाँसिरहेका थियौ

You were laughing.
तिमी हाँसिरहेकी थियौ

Third Person

She was laughing.　They were laughing.
त्यो हाँसिरहेकी थिई　तिनीहरू हाँसिरहेका थिए

She was laughing.
तिनी हाँसिरहेकी थिइन्

(vi) **Past Perfect Tense** (पूर्ण भूतकाल)

(Masculine Subject—कर्ता पुलिंग)

Second Person

Singular　　　　　Plural
Thou hadst laughed.　You had laughed.
तैं हाँसेका थिइस　तिमीहरू हाँसेका थियौ

You had laughed
तिमी हाँसेका थियौ

Third Person

He had laughed.
त्यो हांसेका थियो

They had laughed.
तिनीहरू हांसेका थिए

He had laughed
तिनी हांसेका थिए

(Feminine Subject—कर्ता स्त्रीलिंग)

Second Person

Thou hadst laughed.
तैं हांसेकी थिइस्

You had laughed.
तिमीहरू हांसेका थियौ

You had laughed.
तिमी हांसेकी थियौ

Third Person

She had laughed.
त्यो हांसेकी थिई

They had laughed.
तिनीहरू हांसेका थिए

She had laughed.
तिनी हांसेकी थिइन्

(vii) Unknown Past Tense (अज्ञात भूत काल)
(Masculine subject—कर्ता पुंलिंग)
Second Person

Singular	Plural
Thou didst happen to laugh.	You happened to laugh.
तैं हांसिछस	तिमीहरू हांसेछौ
You happened to laugh.	
तिमी हांसेछौ	

Third Person

He happened to laugh.

त्यो हाँसिछ

He happened to laugh.

तिनी हाँसेछन

They happened to laugh.

तिनीहरू हाँसेछन

(Feminine Subject—कर्ता स्त्रीलिंग)
Second Person

Singular	Plural
Thou didst happen to laugh.	You happened to laugh.
तैं हाँसिछस	तिमीहरू हाँसेछौ
You happened to laugh.	
तिमी हाँसिछ्यौ	

Third Person

She happened to laugh.

त्यो हाँसिछ

She happened to laugh.

तिनी हाँसिछन

They happened to laugh.

तिनीहरू हाँसेछन

(viii) Future Indefinite Tense

(सामान्य भविष्यत् काल)

(Masculine Subject—कर्ता पुलिंग)

Second Person

Singular	Plural

Thou wilt laugh·
तैं हांस्नेछस्

You will laugh
तिमीहरू हांस्नेछौ

You will laugh.
तिमी हांस्नेछौ

Third Person

He will laugh
त्यो हांस्नेछ

They will laugh.
तिनीहरू हांस्नेछन्

He will laugh.
तिनी हांस्नेछन्

(Feminine Subject — कर्ता स्त्रीलिंग)

Second Person

Singular	Plural

Thou wilt laugh.
तैं हांस्नेछस्

You will laugh.
तिमीहरू हांस्नेछौ

You will laugh.
तिमी हांस्नेछौ

Third Person

She will laugh.
त्यो हांस्नेछ

They will laugh.
तिनीहरू हांस्नेछन

She will laugh.
तिनी हाँस्नेछ

(ix) Future Perfect Tense (पूर्ण भविष्यत काल)

(Masculine Subject—कर्ता पुलिंग)

Second Person

Thou wilt have laughed.
तैं हांसेको हुनेछस्

You will have laughed.
तिमीहरू हांसेका हुनेछौ

You will have laughed.
तिमी हांसेका हुनेछौ

Third Person

Singular	Plural
He will have laughed.	They will have laughed.
त्यो हांसेका हुनेछ	तिनीहरू हांसेका हुनेछन
He will have laughed.	
तिनी हांसेका हुनेछन्	

(Feminine Subject—कर्ता स्त्रीलिंग)

Second Person

Thou wilt have laughed.
तैं हांसेकी हुनेछस्

You will have laughed.
तिमीहरू हांसेका हुनेछौ

You will have laughed.
तिमी हांसेकी हुनेछौ

Third Person

She will have laughed.
त्यो हाँसिको हुनेछ

They will have laughed.
तिनीहरू हांसेका हुनेछन

She will have laughed.
तिनी हासेकी हुनेछन

(x) Future Conditional Tense
(संभावना भविष्यत् काल)

(Masculine Subject — कर्ता पुलिंग)

Second Person

Thou wilt laugh.
तं हाँस्लास्

You will laugh
तिमीहरू हांसौला, हाँस्लाउ

You will laugh.
तिमी हाँस्लाउ, हांसौला

Third Person

Singular	Plural
He will laugh.	They will laugh.
त्यो हाँस्ला	तिनीहरू हाँस्लान्
He will laugh.	
तिनी हाँस्लान्	

(Feminine Subject — कर्ता स्त्रीलिंग)
Second Person

Thou wilt langh.
तं हाँस्लिस

You will laugh.
तिमीहरू हाँसौला

You will laugh.
तिमी हांसौली, हाँस्लेउ

Third Person

He will laugh.
र्यो हाँस्ली

They will laugh.
तिनीहरू हाँस्लान्

He will laugh.
तिनी हाँस्लिन

Habitual Tense — अभ्यासबोधक काल
(abhyasbodhak kal)

The Habitual Tense is used to denote an action to which somebody is habituated. The verb is formed according to the number and gender of the nominative by adding गर to the root.

The Habitual Present, Future and Past Tenses are to be formed in the following manner:

Present (Masculine Subject)

Singular

1st

Plural

I use to laugh
म हाँस्ने गछूँ

We use to laugh.
हामी हाँस्ने गछोँ

2nd

Thou usest to laugh.
तँ हाँस्ने गछुंस

You use to laugh.
तिमीहरू हाँस्ने गछौँ

3rd

He uses to laugh.
र्यो हास्ने गछ

They use to laugh.
तिनीहरू हाँस्ने गछंन्

Future (Masculine Subject)

1st

I shall be laughing.
म हांस्ने गर्ह्रॉला

We shall be laughing.
हामी हांस्ने गरौंला

2nd

Thou wilt be laughing.
तैं हाँस्ने गर्लास्

You will be laughing.
तिमी हांस्ने गरौला

3rd

He will be laughing.
त्यो हांस्ने गर्ला

They will be laughing.
तिनीहरू हांस्ने गलान

Past (Masculine Subject)

1st

I used to laugh.
म हांस्नेगर्थें

We used to laugh.
हामी हांस्ने गर्थ्यौं

2nd

Thou didst use to laugh.
तैं हांस्ने गर्थिस्

You used to laugh.
तिमी हांस्नु गर्थ्यौं

3rd

He used to laugh.
त्यो हांस्ने गर्थ्यों

They used to laugh.
तिनीहरू हांस्नै गर्थें

Nominative Case-ending (ले — le)

The case-ending ले is added to the subject of a transitive verb in the Present Perfect, Past

Indefinite. Past Perfect, Unknown Past, Future Perfect and Conditional Indefinite Tenses ; as :—

I have eaten.—मैंले खाएको छु

I ate—मैंले खाएँ

I had eaten—मैंले खाएको थिए

I happened to eat—मैंले खाएछु

I shall have eaten—मैंले खाएको हुनेछु

If you eat – तिमीले खाए

This case-ending (ले) is not added to the subject of an intransitive verb.

Exercise

1. Correct the following by showing reasons :

म एउटी लडकौलाई देखें । उसले घर गयो । सीता हाँसिरहेको छ । म घर गएको थियो । भारतीले दौडेर ब्राई । बहिनी हांस्नेछिन् । श्यामले किताब किनि छ ।

2.   Translate into Nepali :—

She happened to purchase a Pen. What things have you bought ? Has he given his book to you? I have seen his brother. Were you drawing a sketch ? I used to walk everyevening. We shall be eating sweets everyday.

LESSON — 17

Uses of Infinitives, Auxillary Verbs, Participles, Imperative and Subjunctive Mood

Kridant, Sahakari Kriya, Vidhyartha and Anischayartha

कृदन्त, सहकारी क्रिया, विध्यर्थ तथा अनिश्चयार्थ

Infinitive (कृदन्त)

The Infinitive is formed by adding 'नु' to a verbroot, e. g. खा+नु= खानु (to eat). जा+नु= जांनु (to go), गर+नु—गनु (to do), etc.

There are two forms of infinitives :—

(i) Simple, and (ii) Inflected.

(i) Simple Infinitive may be used in five different ways :—

(a) As subject to a verb ;—

To walk in the morning is good for health—
सबेरै डुल्नु स्वास्थ्यको लागि अ्रसल छ

To laugh too much is not good—धेरै हांस्नु ठीक
छैन

156

(b) To denote honour, added to the third person singular form of हुनु (to be) :—

My father went—बा जानुभयो

The teacher teaches - गुरु पढाउनुहुन्छ

(c) In the sense of duty or necessity to be followed by पर्छं (should) :—

You should do this work—तिमीले यो काम गर्नु पर्छं

Panjabis should learn Nepali— पंजाबीहरूले नेपाली सिक्नु पर्छं

(d) As object to the prepositions :—

To fear to die—मर्नु देखि डराउनु

Expert to speak – बोल्नुमा शिपालु

(e) As object to a verb :—

He said what he had to say— आफ्नो भन्नु भन्यो

(ii) Inflected infinitive may be used in three different senses ;—

(a) To denote a purpose ।—

He goes there to work—उ त्यहां गर्नु जान्छ

I have come here to see you— म यहाँ तिमीलाई भेट्नु आएको हुँ

(b) To denote a special sense :—

Ram did his level best— रामले गर्नु गर्यो

Hari said what he should not—हरिले भन्नु नभन्नु
भन्यो

(c) With the verbs लाग्नु, दिनु, पाउनु :—

He began to eat—त्यो खानु लाग्यो

Why have you allowed him to come here—
उसलाई यहाँ किन आउन दिएको ?

I could not go to the meeting—म सभामा जान
पाइन

N. B.—The infinite-ending नु is sometimes
changed into न.

Auxiliary Verbs

हुनु, पनुँ, जानु, गनुँ, हिंड्नु, रहनु, सक्नु, हाल्नु, दिनु, राख्नु,
छोड्नु, लाउनु etc. are used as auxiliary verbs to sup-
plement the principal verb. Sometimes they are
used as principal verbs also ; as :—

I can see—म देख्न सक्छु

He can do—त्यो गर्न सक्छ

You will not be able to do—तिमी गर्न सक्तैनौ

I began to tell - मले भन्न लागें

He began to go—त्यो जान लाग्यो

How have you got hurt—तपाईलाई चोट कसरी लाग्यो

I want to go—म जान चाहन्छु

What do you want to do—तिमी के गर्न चाहन्छौ

What do you want—तिमी के चाह छौ ?

Let him speak—उसलाई भन्न देऊ

Let me go now—मलाई अब जान देऊ

What do you give—तिमी के दिन्छौ ?

He could not see me—उसले मलाई भेटन पाएन

He could not go there—त्यो त्यहां जान पाएन

We have got ten rupees—हामीले दश रूपेयाँ पायौं

He has finished the work—त्यसले काम गरिसकेको छ

I have taken my meal—मैले खाना खाइसकेको छु

He has spent all his property—उसले सब सम्पति
सक्यो

Go on writing—लेख्तै जाऊ

Raj is telling—राज भन्देगइरहेछ

The boy went home—लडको घर घयो

He had to go home—उसलाई घर जान्नु परयो

He should work—उसले काम गर्नु पछ

Kumar won the lottery—कुमारलाई चिट्ठा परयो

I will do it—म यो काम गरिछोडछु

Tenzing climbed to the peak—तेन्जिडले टुप्पामा
पुगिछोडयो

I shall give it up—म यसलाई छोडछु

The auxiliary verbs are generally used in-
transitively (when they are supplementary), but

in case of verbs दिनु, चाहनु, खोज्नु, पाउनु, लाउनु they are used transitively ; as ;

He did not allow me to go – उसले मलाई जान दिएन

I wanted to go – मैले जान खोजें

He wanted to say—उसले भन्न चाह्यो

Shyam could not eat—श्यामले खान पाएन

Cause him to say— उसलाई भन्न लाऊ

Participles

In Nepali there are three kinds of Participles viz ; (i) Present Participle, (ii) Past Participle. (iii) Conjunctive Participle.

(i): The Present Participle is formed by adding दै, दो, एर or इरहेको to the root of a verb ; as :—

दगुर + दै = दगुर्दै (running)

नाच + दो = नाच्दो (dancing)

हाँस + एर = हांसेर (laughing)

खा + इरहेको = खाइरहेको (eating)

It is used :—

(a) To qualify a Noun or Pronoun like an adjective or to modify a verb like an an adverb ; as :—

The running child fell down— दगुरिरहेको बालक लोट्यो

The girl fled away laughing — हाँस्द लडकी भागी

(b) To denote continuation of an action ; as :—

The boy chewing gram sat on the chair.
लडका चना चपाउँदे मेचमा बस्यो

The girl was dancing as she sang — त्यो लडकी गाएर नाच्थी

(c) To denote immediate completion of an action ; as :—

As soon as he heard my voice, he cried aloud — मेरो आवाज सुनेर त्यो चिल्लायो

After saying this he went away — यति भनेर त्यो गयो

N. B. Continuation of action may be denoted by the repetition of the Present Participle ending in दै ; as :—

In course of walk we got tired — हिड्दा-हिड्दै हामी थाक्यौं

While going on we took notice of him — जाँदा जाँदै हामीले उसलाई देख्यौं

(ii) The Past Participle is formed by adding एको to the root of a verb ; as :—

पढ्+एको = पढेको (read)

लेख्+एको = लेखेको (written)

It is used :—

(1) to qualify a noun ; as : –

Where is the well-read man – पढे-लेखेको मानिस
कहाँ छ

The woman sitting on is blind— बसे की श्राइमाई
अन्धी छ

Why are you spoiling the work done— गरेको
काम किन बिगाछौं

(b) To denote an action done in the past ;
as :—

Forget the past —बितेकोलाई बिसिदेऊ

Mend what is broken—बिग्रेको बनाऊ

(iii) The conjunctive Participle is formed by
adding दा, एर etc. to the root of the verb ; as :—

सुन्+दा = सुन्दा (hearing)

भन्+एर = भनेर (saying)

It is used :—

(a) for a Participle like 'taking' ; as :—

Going there I saw everything—त्यहाँ गएर मैले सब देखें

(b) for an Adverbial phrase like 'having taken' ; as :—

Having taken his meal he went to take rest—खाना खाएर त्यो आराम लिन गयो

Having seen me he stopped – मलाई देखेर त्यो अडयो

Having heard this I got surprised—यो सुन्दा म चकित भएँ

Imperative mood

(विध्यर्थ—Vidhyartha)

The imperative Mood expresses an order. It is used only in the Present Tense, and only in the Second person ; as :—

Singular	Plural
Laugh or laugh thou.	Laugh or laugh you
हाँस	हाँस

The Imperative mood is formed :—

(a) by the root verb itself in the Singular Number and by adding '**अ**' to it in the Plural Number, if it ends in हलन्त (ृ) ; as :—

बस

Singular	Plural
Sit or sit thou.	Sit or sit you.
वस्	बस

(b) by adding ई, in the Singular Number and ए, in the Plural to the root verb if it ends in अ or उ ; as :—

पक्र

Singular	Plural
Catch or catch thou.	Catch or catch you.
पक्री	पक्रे

कुहू

Singular	Plural
Rot or rot thou.	Rot or rot you.
कुही	कुहे

(c) by the root verb itself in the Singular Number and by adding 'ओ' to it in the Plural Number, if it ends in आ ; as :—

जा

Singular	Plural
Go or go thou.	Go or go you.
जा	जाओ

N. B. The respectful Imperative in the Singular Number is formed by adding 'ऊ' to the root ; as :—जाऊ (go), लॆजाऊ (take), खाऊ (eat), etc.

(d) by changing उ into ओ in the Singular and than adding ओ in the Plural if the root ending in उ is single-lettered ; as :—

धु

Singular	Plural
Wash or wash thou.	Wash or wash you.
धो	धोओ

N. B. The respectful Imperative in the Singular Number is formed by adding 'ऊ' to the already changed form of ओ ; as :—धोऊ (wash), होऊ (be), रोऊ (weep), etc.

(e) by dropping the last letter in the Singular Number and by replacing it by ग्रो in the Plural, if the root verb ends in the pure vowel उ ; as : —

गाउ

Singular	Plural
Sing or sing thou.	Sing or sing you.
गा	गाग्रो

N.B The respectful Imperative in the Singular Number is formed by replacing उ by ऊ ; as : —

गाऊ (sing), पाऊ (get), ख्याऊ (row), etc.

The singular Imperative of the verb ग्राउ is also formed as ग्राइज (come).

(f) by changing इ into ए in the Singular and then adding ग्रो in the Plural if the root verb ends in इ ; as : —

उभि

Singular	Plural
Stand or stand thou.	Stand or stand you.
उभि	उभिग्रो, उभिग्रो

'‍नू' (In the imperative)

When नू is used to denote imperative sense no change is made in the root irrespective of gender, number and person of the subject, but only that the subject is suffixed by ले ; as :—

तैंले or तिमीले हाँस्नू, बस्नू, पक्रनू, जानू, घुन्नू, गाउन्नू, दिन्नू, उभिन्नू, etc.

एस, ए (In the imperative)

The imperative mood in the second person is formed by adding एस in the singular number and ए in the plural as well but only when the action implied through the verb is expected to be done not in the presence of the speaker ; as :—

Singular	Plural
उभिएस	उभिए
गायस	गाए
हाँसिएस	हाँसे
धोएस	धोए
कुहेस	कुहे
दिएस	दिए
बसेस	बसे

In respect of the verb जा. however, the form is changed into ग when एस् or ए is added ; as :—

गएस   गए

Respectful Imperative

The pronoun तैं (thou) is used only in addressing children. menials, dearly beloved persons and God तिमी (you) is the common term used between equals. or in addressing somebody lower in honorific sense. The respectful imperatives illustrated above are used to request such a person. तपाईं or यहाँ (you) is used for other than intimate or respecrful persons higher in rank, relation or position, than the speaker. It is formed by adding होस् or होला the infinitive. The former is used to denote a request to be carried out in the present, while the latter in future ; as :—

Please sit down—बस्नु होस

You will please sit down—बस्नु होला

Other Persons of the Imperative

To express the First and Third persons of the Imperative mood, we add ऊ (singular) and औं (plural), and ओस (singular) and ऊन् (plural) to the

root verb in the First and Third Persons respectively ; as :—

Person	Singular	Plural
	बस	
1st Person	बसूँ	बसौं
3rd Person	वसोस	बसून्
	कुहु	
1st Person	कुहूँ	कुहौं
3rd Person	कुहोस्	कुहून्
	पक्र	
1st Person	पक्रू	पक्रौं
3rd Person	पक्रोस	पक्रून्
	जा	
1st Person	जाऊँ	जाब्रौं
3rd Person	जाब्रोस	जाऊन्
	धु	
1st Person	धोऊँ	थोब्रौं
3rd Person	धोब्रोस्	धोऊन्
	गाउ	
1st Person	गाऊँ	गाब्रौं
3rd Person	गाब्रोस	गाऊन्
	दि	
1st Person	दिऊँ	दिब्रौं
3rd Person	दिब्रोस	दिऊन्

Person	Singular	Plural
	उभि	
Ist Person	उभिऊँ	उभिग्रौं
3rd Person	उभिग्रोस्	उभिऊन्

Exercise

1. Correct the following : –

म हेनैं सक्छु । रामलाई पक्र । तैं धुनू । म जानुपछं । त्यहां जाएर मैंले सब देखे । मेचमाथि उमैं ।

2. Translate into Nepali :—

I saw him. Don't come here. Let me go there. I saw her singing. Please do this work. He may come. You should do every work. We began to say but he did not hear. What should you do ? Do what you can do. He has eaten all. They could not do. I can do nothing for you. Why are you spoiling the work done before.

———

LESSON—18

Voice

(वाच्य—Vachya)

Voice is a form of speech denotes whether the subject or the object of a verb is prominent in the sentence. In Nepali ; There are three kinds of voice ; as :—

(1) कर्तृवाच्य (Active Voice).

(2) कर्मवाच्य (Passive Voice).

(3) भाववाच्य (Impersonal Voice).

(1) कर्तृवाच्य—In the Active Voice the Subject is prominent in the sentence ; as :—

Yadav reads a book—यादव किताब पढछ

Swarn plucks a flower—स्वर्ण फूल टिप्छे

(2) कर्मवाच्य—In the Passive Voice the object is prominent in the sentence. The verb is formed by adding इ to the Past Tense and the subject takes the case-ending बाट (from), and the verb is formed according to the number, gender and person of the object ; as :—

171

A book is read by Ram—रामबाट किताब पढिन्छ

Flowers are plucked by Swarn—स्वर्णं बाट फूल टिपिन्छ

(3) In the Impersonal Voice the verb is always intransitive and ?stands neither with the subject nor with the object. It remains always in the third person, singular number and neuter gender ; as :—

I am unable to move—मबाट हिंडिंदैन

He went—उसबाट गइयो

N. B. The verbs जा (to go), हु (to be) and लैजा (to take) when changed into impersonal voice take both the forms of जाइन्छ and गइन्छ ; होइन्छ and भइन्छ ; लगिन्छ and लैजाइन्छ in the present tense. and only one form of गइयो, गइएको छ ; गइएथ्यो, गइएछ ; भइयो, भइएछ and लगिया, लगिएथ्यो in the past tenses.

A few examples of Active (कर्तृं), Passive (कर्म) and Impersonal (भाव) voice are give below :—

Active Voice	Passive Voice
कर्तृं वाच्य	कर्मवाच्ठ
मैंले किताब लेखें (I wrote a book.)	मबाट किताब लेखियो
तिमीले ग्रन्थ पढ्यो (You read books.)	तिमीबाट ग्रन्थ पढिए

Actiue Voice	Passive Voice
कर्तृ वाच्य	कर्मवाच्य

म रोटी खान्छु (I eat bread.)	मबाट रोटी खाइन्छ
त्यो फल खान्छ (He eats fruit.)	त्यसबाट फल खाइन्छ
म चिट्ठी लेख्छु (I write a letter.)	मबाट चिट्ठी लेखिन्छ
त्यो मलाई देख्छ (He sees me.)	त्यसबाट म देखिन्छु

Exercise

Change the voice of :—

तं काम गर्छस् । त्यो किताब पढ्छ । उसव'ट किताब लेखियो । तिनीहरू गोत सुन्छन् । रामले सीतालाई देखे । मैले फलफूल खाएको थिएं । शाम सुत्छ । शीला दगुछें । सीता पौडि लेल्छिन् ।

LESSON—19

Conversation in Nepali

(नेपालीमा कुराकानी)

Teacher—What is your name ?
शिक्षक—तिम्रो नाम के हो ?

Mohan—My name is Mohan.
मोहन—मेरो नाम मोहन हो ।

Teacher—What's your father's name ?
शिक्षक—तिम्रो पिताजीको नाम के हो ?

Mohan—My father's name is Divyaman Mul.
मोहन—मेरो पिताजीको नाम दिव्यमान मूल हो ।

Teacher—What does he do ?
शिक्षक—उहाँ के काम गनुं हुन्छ ?

Mohan—He is a businessman.
मोहन—उहाँ बेपार गनुं हुन्छ ।

Teacher—What's your birth-place ?
शिक्षक—तिम्रो जन्मस्थान कहाँ हो ?

Mohan—My birth-place is Bhaktapur.
मोहन—मेरो जन्मस्थान भक्तपुर हो ।

174

Teacher—Where are you living now ?

शिक्षक—अहिले तिमीहरू कहाँ बस्छौ ?

Mohan—Now we are living in Kathmandu.

मोहन—अहिले हामीहरू काठमाडौं बस्छौं ।

Teacher—Who else are living at your house ?

शिक्षक – तिम्रो घरमा अरु को को छन् ?

Mohan—There are my mother, my younger
brother and two sisters at our house.

मोहन – मेरी आमा, मेरो भाइ र दुइ बहिनी ।

Ram– Is this no. 50 ?

राम   के यो नम्बर पचास हो ?

Shyam—Does Mr. Gopi live here ?

श्याम—के गोपीज्यू यहीं बस्नुहुन्छ ?

Surendra—No, sir, he does not live here. He
lives in the next house.

सुरेन्द्र – अहँ, यहाँ बस्नुहुन्न, त्यो संगेको घरमा बस्नुहुन्छ ।

Ramman—(Going to the next house) Is Mr.
Gopi at home ?

राममान—(संगेको घरमा गएर) गोपीज्यू हुनुहुन्छ ?

Dwarika—No, he is not in   He is out.

द्वारिका—अहँ, हुनुहुन्न, बाहिर जानु भएको छ ।

Dhirendra — Out of Kathmandu or here to see some body ?

धिरेन्द्र—काठमाडौंबाट नै बाहिर हो कि यहीं कसँलाई भेट्न ?

Dwarika — No, he is here that he has gone to meet some friend

द्वारिका— होइन, यहीं कसँलाई भेट्न ।

Ramman— When do you expect him back ?

राममान—कहिले सम्ममा फर्कनु होला ?

Dwarika—He is expected even now.

द्वारिका - आउँदै हुनु होला ।

Dhirendra—All right, we shall wait for some time.

धिरेन्द्र   हुन्छ त, केहो बेर बाटो हेरौं ।

Dwarika—Do you like to sit in the varandah or come inside the room ?

द्वारिका— तपाई हरू दलानमं वस्नुहुन्छ कि मित्र कोठामा आउनुहुन्छ ?

Ramman—No, thank you. We shall prefer to sit here in the varandah.

राममान— होइन, धन्यवाद छ । यहीं दलानमं ठीक छ ।

Dwarika— Here is a newspaper. You may read it if you like.

द्वारिका—यो अखबार हो । तपाई हरू पढ्न सक्नु हुन्छ ।

Dhirendra --Thank you. If you don't mind a
glass of water, please.

घिरेन्द्र—धन्यवाद । तपाई लाई कष्ट हुँदैनभने एक गिलास पानी···

Dwarika—Certainly, I am getting a glass of
sharbat.

द्वारिका—प्रबश्य, म शरबत ल्याउँछु ।

Dhirendra—No, no, thank you. Only plain
water will do.

घिरेन्द्र—होइन, होइन । खाली पानी ल्याइदिनुहोस्

Ramman –It is too late, we can't wait any
more.

राममान—घेरै वेर भइसक्यो, प्रब हामी पर्खन सक्तैनौं ।

Dhirendra—Sir, please do one thing ; convey
our message to him.

घिरेन्द्र – महाशय, तपाई एउटा काम गरि दिनुहुन्छ कि ? हाम्रो
खबर वहाँलाई भनिदिनु होला ।

Dwarika—Oh yes, very gladly. Have you got
your card ?

द्वारिका--जरूर, खुशीसाथ । तपाई हरूसंग कार्ड छ ?

Ramman —No sir, but will you please give us a
piece of paper and a pen or pencil ?

राममान – अहँ, छैन, तर तपाई हामीलाई एक टुका कागज र कलम
प्रथवा पिन्सिल दिन सक्नु होला ?

Dwarika—Here is paper and a pencil.

द्वारिका—लिनुहोस् कागज र पिन्सिल ।

Ramman—Thank you.

राममान—धन्यवाद ।

Dhirendra—Please give this paper to him
when he returns.

धिरेन्द्र—जब जहाँ फर्कनु होला कृपा गरी उहांलाई यो कागज दिनु
होला ।

Ramman—Thank you very much for your
kindness.

राममान - तहाईको दयाको लागि तपाईं लाई धेरैं धेरैं धन्यवाद,
नमस्ते ।

Dhirendra—But don't forget to give him this
paper.

धिरेन्द्र—तर वहांलाई यो कागज दिन नविर्संनु होला ।

Dwarika—No, sir. I shall not forget.

द्वारिका—कहाँ बिसंन्थें, बिसंन्न ।

LESSON—20

Specimens of Translation

(अनुवादको नमूना)

(1)

एउटा काग तीर्खाले मानौं मर्नें लागेको थियो । उसले एउटा गाग्रो देख्यो जसको पींधमा केही पानी थियो । दुर्भाग्यवश उसले आफ्नो चुच्चो पानीसम्म पुन्याउन सकेन । उसले अनेक बाजी कोशिश गन्यो तर सफल हुन सकेन । त्यसपछि उसले त्यो गाग्रोलाई नै घोप्ट्याइ दिनु कोशिश गर्यो यसकारणले कि पानी पिउन सकियोस् । तर त्यो त्यत्तिको बलियो पनि थिएन !

A crow was almost dying of thirst. It found a pitcher which had a little water at the bottom. Unfortunately the crow was not able to take its bill into the water Again and again it tried but to no effect. Than it tried to turn the pitcher over, so that might get the water But it was not strong enough for this.

179

ऊँट पानी नखाइकन कैथ्यौं दिन हिड्न सक्तछ । उसको पेटमा पानीका
थैलीहरू हुन्छन् जसमा ऊ चार पाँच दिनसम्मलाई पुग्ने गरी पानी भ
सक्तछ । ऊँटले टाढाबाट सुँघेर पानो पत्ता लगाउन सक्तछ र अगाड़ि बढे
पानी भेट्टाउँछ । अग्नि त्यो खूब पानी पिउँन्छ, सवार पनि उत्रन्छ । पान
पिउँन्छ र आपनो छालाको घोक्री भर्दछ ।

The camel can travel for days together withou
water.   Its stomach is filled with water cells i
which it can store up a sufficient quantity to las
it for four or five days.   The camel smells wate
from a long distance and goes on and on till i
comes up to it.   Then it drinks sufficiently an
the rider also comes down, drinks water and fil
his leather bag with it.

LESSON—21

Passages For Translation

(अनुवादको लागि लेखांश)

I

Translate into English :—

(1)

घोडा एउटा राम्रो पशु हो । त्यो धेरै काम लाग्ने हुन्छ । त्यसका चार खुट्टा छन् । त्यसको गर्दनमा रौं (mane) हुन्छ । त्यो धेरै छिटो दगुर्न सक्छ । मानिस त्यसलाई चढ्छन् । मेरो घोडा तिम्रो घोडाभन्दा असल छ ।

(2)

एउटा बूढो र उसको छोरो दुवै परदेशमा थिए । उनीहरूसंग एउटा गधा पनि थियो । गधामाथि आफ्नो भारी लादेर बाबु-छोरा दुवै हिंडिरहेका थिए । मानिसहरूले यो देखेर भने—'हेर, यो कस्ता पागल हुन् ! गधा मै-मै कन पनि पैदल हिंड्छन् ।" यो सुनेर बूढो गधामाथि सवार भयो ! अलि टाढा गएका थिएनन् मानिसहरूले भने—'हेर हेर, कस्ता निर्दयो बाबु ! आफू गधा चढेर छोरोलाई हिंहाउँछ । यो सुनेर बाबु गधाबाट उभ्यो । छोरोलाई चढायो ।

181

(3)

राम एक दश वर्षको केटो हो । त्यो पांचौं कक्षामा पद्दछ । त्योसग एउटा राम्रो तस्वीर छ । त्यसलाई ऊ खूब जतन गरेर राख्तछ । उतको बाबुले किताब किन्न उसलाई दश रुपैयां दिएका छन् । त्यो पसलमा जान्छ ।

II

Translate into Nepali :—

(1)

Lal Bahadur had three sons. They were Ram, Shyam and Hari. Hari was the youngest (कान्छो) and Ram was the eldest (जेठो) of all. Hari was ten years old and Ram twenty seven years. Lal Bahadur had lost his wife five years back.

(2)

Men and beasts have limbs. A man has two arms and two hands, two legs and two feet. A lamb has four legs. A dog has four paws. A cow has cloven hoofs. Birds have no teeth. We went to pay a visit to the zoological gardens. We were greatly delighted to see various large animals.

————

LESSON—22

Idioms & Proverbs

(बाक्पद्धति र उखान)

A group of words which have a special meaning when used together, is called in idiom (वाक्-पद्धति).

A group of words which have a complete sense of a short wise saying commonly used by the people is called a proverb (उखान).

The expression becomes appropriate and forceful by using idioms and proverbs. Idioms and proverbs are used in Nepali literature and conversation, so the learners should know the correct use of them. The following is a list of some idioms and proverbs.

Idioms

आज आज भोलि भोलि भनीं टार्नु —to evade.

आगो फोस्नु —to incite to quarrel.

आँखा झिम्क्याउनु—to make a gesture with eyes.

आँखा टूलो गनु—to frighten.

अवसर चुक्नु—to miss the chance.

आँखा चिम्लनु—to neglect.

गोडा पनु—to surrender.

खुट्टा पनु—to surrender.

कान पक्रनु—to accept one's folly.

कागत गनु—to sign a legal document.

कपाल फोनु—to make a level best.

ओठ टोक्नु—to be thoughtful.

म्यालु खानु—to fail.

उल्ली बिल्ली खेलाउनु—to befool one.

दिन पर दिन—day by day.

दाउ लाग्नु—to get an opportunity.

दाह्रा किट्नु—to grind teeth with rage.

चुरोट खानु—to smoke.

चाल चल्नु—to play a device.

घर फोड्नु—to create disturbances in the family.

गुन लाउनु—to help in need.

जस्तालाई तस्तै—tit for tat.

दिल बस्नु—to be in love with.

दृष्टि पुर्‍याउनु—to be careful.

दुहाइ दिनु—to call for help.

दिल दिनु—to fall in love.

नाक चेप्य्राउनु—to be displeased.

नाता तोड्नु—to sever relations.

निमकको सोझो गर्नु—to be loyel to the employer.

पट्टल बन्द गर्नु—to close eyes.

पेट पोल्नु—to be jealous.

सांचो बोल्नु   to speak the truth.

साथ दिनु—to help.

बचन दिनु—to commit.

म्याद पुग्नु   to come to end of life.

मौका छोप्नु—to avail of the chance

मनमानी खुशीराजीसंग—according to one's sweet will.

मनको लड्डुको पूल बांध्नु—to build castles in the air.

मतलब पुर्‍याउनु—to serve one's end.

बगली मार्नु—to pick pocket.

फन्दामा पर्नु—to fall into difficulty.

पेटमा आगो बल्नु—to be extremely hungry.

हँसी उडाउनु—to laugh at.

हर तरह गर्नु—to try every means.

हात जोड्नु—to salute.

हातको सफाई—legerdemain. jugglery.

हवामा कुरा गर्नु—to talk uselessly.

Proverbs

आफू भलो त जगतै भलो—Good mind good find.

आफ्नो आफ कोयाको दाम—Earth's joys and heaven's combined.

औसर अउँछ पर्खं दैन –Time and tide wait for none.

कुकुरको पुच्छर बाह्र बर्ष ढुगामा हाले पनि बांगाबांगे — Black will take no other hue.

एक पन्थ दो काज—To kill two birds with one shot.

अन्धा देशको कानै राजा—A figure among ciphers.

आज मर्यो मोलि आेखती—To treat after death.

कानो देशमा आंखा चिम्लनु, लंगडा देशमा खुट्टा उल्चानु Do in Rome as Roma's do.

कुम्हालेको हातको माटो—The potter has his power over his clay.

खाने वहादुरलाई जुगाले छेक्तिन Where there is will there is a way

गर्जने मेघ बर्षंदैन—Barking dogs seldom bite.

घमण्डीको शिर निचा— Pride has its fall.

ङाउ गर्दा अगि सनेंको—Who will bell the cat ?

चार दिनको चांदनी फेरि क्षंध्यारो रात—A nine days' wonder.

जस्तै देश उस्तै भेष—When at Rome do as a Roman. does.

जसको तरवार उसको दरवार—Might is right.

जस्ता राजा उस्तै प्रजा—As the king is so are the subject.

जस्तो बोट उस्तै फूल—Like father like son.

दालमा कालो छ—There is something black in it.

धनले धन कमाउँछ—Money begets money.

घोबी को कुकुर घर को न घाटको—Neither fish nor fowl.

नाच्न जाने आंगन टेढ़ो A bad workman quarrels with his tools.

मियाँको दौड मस्जीदसम्म—The priest goes no further from the church.

मुखमा राम राम बगलोमा छूरा—A wolf in a lamb's skin,

लोभले पाप, पापले ताप—No vice like avarice.

सवभन्दा जाति चूप Silence is golden.

सर्पलाई दूध—To cherish a serpent in one's bosom.

सास छउञ्जेल को आस—While there's life there is hope.

सेवा गरे मेवा पाइन्छ—No pain, no gain.

हुने बिरवाको चिल्लो पात—Morning shows the day.

Examples

मानसिले सबै कुरामा दृष्टि पुरयाउनु पर्छ—Man should be careful in everything.

उसको मुद्दा को श्राज पनि टुग्गा लागेन   His case could not
                                be decided even to-day.

सोझो कुरा मम – Speak the truth.

रामले हरि को साथ दिएन – Ram did not help Hari.

रातो पुष्ट गोलमेंडा एउटा देख्ता मेरो जिब्रो रसायो – At the

sight of red round tomato my mouth began to
                                              water.

तिमी किन हरेक कुरामा नाक फुल उँछौ – Why are you
                                puffed by every word ?

———

LESSON—23

LETTER WRITING & CORRESPONDENCE

(चिट्ठी लेख्नु)

Letters are of different classes, as :—

   (i)   घरायशी पत्र (Private letters).

  (ii)   कामकाजी पत्र (Business letters)

 (iii)   निम्तो पत्र (Invitation letters).

  (iv)   वधाई पत्र (Letters of congratulation).

   (v)   समवेदना पत्र (Letters of condolence).

  (vi)   परिचय पत्र (Introductory letters).

 (vii)   अड्डाखानाको पत्र (Official letters).

(viii)   विन्तिपत्र (Petition).

This frame work of letter consists of several parts ; as :—

   (i)   Heading of the letter (writer's address and date —ठेगाना र मिति) ।

  (ii)   Greeting or solution (अभिवादन या सम्बोधन) ।

 (iii)   Contents (बेहोरा) ।

(iv) Conclusion or subscription (आखिरी अंश आपनो सहि समेत) ।

(v) Name and address of the person written to (चिट्ठी पाउनेको नाम र ठेगाना) ।

1. The heading of the letter should be on the right top of the paper ; as :—

मखन टोल,

पाल्पा ।

१६ भद्र, २०३४

2. Begin your letter by greeting or soluting the person you write to on the left hand side a little below the heading.

पूज्य मुमाज्यू !

चरणमा सादर प्रणाम !

Or,

चिरञ्जीवी भाइ त्रिरत्न !

शुभाशीर्वाद !

Or

पूज्य दाज्यूज्यू !

सादर दण्डवत् !

In this way पूज्य, पूजनीय, पूज्या, पूजनीया, etc. are

used in case of letters written to one's **father,**
mother or highly regarded superiors. माननीय,
माननीया, etc. are used to superiors or respectable
persons in general. In equal status the use of
प्यारा, प्रिय, प्रियवर, etc are common. When writing
to juniors or affectionate ones (younger in age)
कल्याणी, चिरजीवी, etc. are used. In business letters,
applications and letters to unknown persons
महोदय, महाशय etc are used.

3. Begin the contents of the letter just below
the salutation and in a new paragraph (i.e. leave
a little space on the left-hand side). In the letter
happens to be a long one, divide it into para-
graphs.

4 Subscription of the letter should be written
at the end of a letter on the right-hand side.

In letters written to superiors आज्ञाकारी is common y used. In letters written to persons of
equal status as well as to juniors and affectionate
once तपाईंको, यहाँको, तिम्रो, भलो चाहने, भवदीय etc are
written.

5. The full name and address of the pers no

should be written on the front side of post cards or envelopes as follows.

(To Superiors or respectable persons).

श्रीमान सुब्बा गोविन्द राज प्रधानको चरणमा माल अड्डा (वोरगज)	टिकट (Stamp)

(To juniors or persons of equal status).

श्रीयुत श्यामकृष्ण भा जनकपुर धाम महोत्तरी	टिकट (Stamp)

If that person happens to live in another person's house or if he is a minor or in case of a woman etc. the name of the head of the family should also be written after 'मार्फत' in the line next to his name.

To Superiors

To whom the letter is written	Greetings	Conclusion and Subscription
Father, teacher uncle, elder brother and other superiors etc.	पूज्य, पूज्यपाद or माननीय दुबाज्यू, मामा दाज्यू गुरु (को चरणमा or सेवामा) etc.	पाउको, हजूरको or यहाँको आज्ञाकारी बालक भानिज, भाइ or शिष्य ..... (को दण्डबत् सेवा etc.
Mother, aunt, elder sister and other superiors etc.	पूज्या, पूज्यपाद or माननीया, सुमाज्यू, माइज्यू, आउज्यू, दिदी (को चरणमा or सेवामा) etc.	

To Persons of Equal Status

Friends	प्रिय मित्र, मित्रवर, प्रियवर, प्रिय साथी etc.	तिम्रो तपाईं को, यहाँको, भलो चाहने, भवदीय etc.

To Juniors

Sons, students, younger brother, cousin, nephew, etc.	चिरंजीवी प्यारा etc.	तिम्रो प्रसल चाहने, भलो चाहने, माया गर्ने etc.

Daughters, niece, younger sisters, etc.	चिरंजीवी, प्यारी etc.	तिम्रो असल चाहने, भलो चाहने, माया गनें etc.

(i) घरायसी पत्र

Private letters may be started in either of the following ways :—

कृपा गरी पठाउनु भएको चिट्ठी समयमै पाएको थिएँ । जबाफ लेखन डिलो हुन गएकोमा कृपया माफ गनुँ होला । (I received the letter you were so kind to send. Please excuse me for delay in replying).

Or

तपाईंको २० गतेको पत्र पाएर आनन्द लाग्यो । (I am glad to receive your letter dated the 20th instant).

(ii) कामकाजी पत्र

Business letters may be started in either of the following ways :—

ठूलो हर्षका साथ सूचना गर्दछु कि तपाईंको २० गतेको चिट्ठी आइपुग्यो । (With great pleasure I inform you that your letter of the 20th instant has arrived).

(iii) निम्तो पत्र

Invitation letter may be written in the following ways :—

यही भद्र २० गते शनिवारको दिन हुने प्रीतिभोजमा यहाँको सुखद उपस्थितिको लागि अनुरोध गर्दछु   (I request you for your happy company at the dinner on Friday, Bhadra 20)

मेरो छोराको व्रतबन्ध हुनाले पाउकष्ट गर्नु मैं मण्डपको शोभा बढाइ दिनु होला भन्ने आशा गर्दछु । (On the occasion of the sacred thread ceremony of my son I hope you will kindly take trouble and enhance the beauty of the building erected for the purpose).

(iv) बधाई पत्र

Letters of congratulation may be started with :

यस्तो शुभ बेलामा मेरो दिलँदेखिको बधाई तथा तिम्रो अति उज्ज्यालो भविष्यको लागि शुभकामना स्वीकार गर्लाउ भन्ने आशा गरेको छु । (I hope on this happy occasion you will accpt my sincere congratulation and good wishes for your brilliant future).

(v) समबेदना पत्र

Letters of condolence may be started with :—

यहाँको महान् बुबाज्यूको स्वर्गवासको दुखद समाचार सुनेर भलाई असाध्य दुःख लाग्यो । (I was extremely sorry to hear the sad news of your revered father's death).

(vi) परिचय पत्र

Introductory letters may be started in the following manners :—

तपाईं संग श्रीमान् श्याम शङ्कर 'श्रान्त' को परिचय गराउन पाउँदा भलाई अपार हर्ष भएको छ । (I am extremely glad to introduce to you Mr. Shyam Shankar 'Shrant').

(vii) अड्डाखानाको पत्र

Official letters may be started with :—

तपाईंको पत्रसंख्या ३३, मिति भाद्र १५, २०३५ को पत्र अनुसार सूचित वर्दछु कि (With reference to your letter no. 33 Dated Bhadra 15, 2035, I beg to inform you that).

(viii) विन्तिपत्र

Petitions may be started with :—

नम्रतापूर्वक निबेदन गर्दछु (Humbly I beg to state).

श्रद्धापूर्वक सूचित गर्दछु (Respectfully I beg to inform you).

Specimens of Some Subscriptions

अरू सब बेसैं छ—Rest is O. K.

शुभकामना सहित—With best wishes.

श्रद्धासहित—With kind regards.

विशेष धन्यदाद—Thanking you.

शीघ्र जबाफको आशामा—Hoping to be favoured with an early reply.

छोटो जबाफको प्रतीक्षामा Awaiting an early reply.

हजूरको प्यारो—Yours affectionately.

हजूरको आज्ञाकारी—Yours obediently.

भवदीय—Yours etc.

तिम्रो भलो चाहने—Your well-wisher.

तिम्रो माया गर्ने—Yours affectionately.

यहाँको or तपाईंको—Yours faithfully

Specimens of Letters

(चिट्ठीको नमुना)

(1)

Letter to a father

३१५, इन्द्रचौक, काठमाडौं
१० भाद्र, २०३४

पूज्य बुबाज्यू,

सादर प्रणाम !

म यहाँ बुधवार दिन सकुशल पुग्नें । मलाई लिन दाज्यू गौचर विमान-घाटमा आइरहनु भएको थियो । मेरो विषय कत्ति चन्दा नलिनु होला । यहाँ सदै बेस छ ।

मुमाको चरणमा सादर प्रणाम, बहिनीलाई आशीर्वाद !

हजूरको प्यारो छोरो
कृष्ण

315, Indrachowk, Kathmandu
10 Bhadra, 2034

Respected father,
   Namaste !

I reached here on wednesday quite safely. My elder brother was present at the Gauchar airport to receive me. Don't be anxious for me. Everything is all right here.

Kindly convey my best respects to my mother and blessings to my sister.

Your affectionate son,
Krishan

(2)

Letter to a friend

ल्यू देहली
१५ माघ, २०३४

प्रिय कृष्ण,

तिम्रो ४ गतेको पत्र पाएँ । बेहोरा पढेर मन साह्रै प्रसन्न भयो । म भोलि बिहानै गाउँतिर हिंड्ने विचार गरेको छु ; आशा छ—तिमी पनि एक हुइ हामामित्र घरतिर आउने छौ ।

तिम्रो साथी,
प्रेम

NEW DELHI
15th Magh, 2034

My dear Krishan

Received your letter of the 4th instant. I was extremely pleased after having read the contents you wrote therein. I intend to go to the village early tomorrow morning and hope that you will also start for home within a week or so.

Your friend,
Prem

(3)

Letter to a book–seller

मेरठ कैन्ट
१५ माघ, २०३४

श्रीयुत प्रबन्धक महोदय,
        रत्न पुस्तक भण्डार, खारी बावली-दिल्ली ।

महोदय,

कृपासाथ तल लेखिएका पुस्तकहरू पार्सल गरेर पठाइदिनु होला । यी पुस्तकको मोल र यिनको पार्सल खर्च समेत मनी रु० ५०/– को नोट यसैसाथ पठाइदिएको छु । उब्रेको रूपैयाँको 'टूलो वर्णमाला' पठाइदिनु होला ।

तपसिल

१. बधूशिक्षा   भानुभक्त आचार्य ।
२: सर्वगुण सम्पन्न कथा—केशवलाल कर्माचार्य ।

३. मुलुक वाहिर—लैनसिह वाङ्गरेल ।

४. नेपालको ऐतिहासिक रूपरेखा—बालचन्द्र शर्मा ।

भवदीय,

किशोर कुमार

Meeruth Cantt.

15 Magh, 2034

To

The Manager,

Ratna Pustak Bhandar, Khari Bawaly Delhi

Dear sir,

Please send the following books by parcel post I am sending Rs. 50/- for their price and postage for the balance if any send "Thulo Varnamala.

List

1. Badhusiksha – By Bhanubhakta Acharya

2. Sarvaguna Sampanna Katha—By Keshavlal Karmacharya.

3. Muluk Bahir—By Lain Singh Bangdel.

4. Nepalko Aitihasik Ruparekha—By Bal Chandra Sharma.

Yours faithfully.

Kishore Kumar

————